The Mole of Moscow

The Ember Enigmas

Book One

Caroline Boxall

Box of Books

Published 4th August 2024

Box of Books Publishing

Front cover by Patrick Knowles at Patrick Knowles Design

Dedication

For my wonderful family: Boxy, Megan, Beth, Emily, Katie, Charlie, Louis, Ryan and Shadow

"It is not the strength of the body that counts, but the strength of the spirit." —— J.R.R. Tolkien

Foreword - Shining a positive light on dementia

'The Mole of Moscow' contains important messages about dementia, focusing on what those living with dementia can still do well, rather on their losses or inabilities. Bravo!

Teepa Snow, Dementia Educator and founder of Positive Approach to Care

Many years ago, my mother-in-law was diagnosed with dementia. It was very sad to see the 'Grandma' we all knew, disappearing before our eyes. When she started to do things which were unsafe, we sadly admitted to ourselves that it was time for her to move to a care home.

Grandma was always a character. She became a different character, but her face always lit up when we visited, even though she couldn't quite remember who we were. We listened to stories about her childhood, some even my husband hadn't heard before. We will never know if the stories were true, but they were entertaining all the same.

From the time Grandma moved into the first care home, up until the day she passed away four years later, she lived with the most extraordinary people. We are a big family, and with seven of us crowding in to visit Grandma, we soon realised that the other residents could be lent a 'spare' visitor to chat with for a few minutes. We got to know the other 'Oldies' as we affectionately called them, and we became very fond of them.

It was tragic that these fine people should be reduced to such shells of their former selves, but they were all magnificent in their own ways. They taught us lessons we could have never learned without having met them, and I am so glad we did. My children understand dementia and how to speak to people who have forgotten everything except for their earliest childhood memories. They have respect for the elderly, no matter how reduced their capacities.

Many of these charming people were the inspiration for "The Oldies".

For Gran, and for all the people who have to get dementia.

Billy
(The Mole of Moscow)

Subscribe

Subscribe to Caroline's blog so you don't miss the next book

For your free book (prequel to *The Mole of Moscow*)
The Secret Young Life of Dmitri Molchalin
sign up to Caroline's website!
www.carolineboxall.com

Hungry for more gripping stories? Explore Caroline's other novels that will keep you turning pages late into the night.
The Runaway Children of Chennai
The Secret Children of Mumbai

Coming soon... **The Fox of Sevastopol**

Contents

One

England, the present

It was the day I found my first clue, something so small yet so significant, and I had no idea of its true importance.

It all began with the old soldier, his medals jingling as he limped through the door, Jude trailing behind and mimicking the limp.

"Our tour now takes us inside the main house," the old man said. "Bletchley Park, the sound of secrecy..."

"...secrecy, secrecy, secrecy," echoed Jude in spiralling whispers. Jude had been his usual annoying and attention-seeking self all morning. He liked to push his luck, but he never knew when to stop.

"Unnamed and uncelebrated, these brave men and women fought a war of their own: the code war," the guide continued. "Cracking Nazi codes, changing the course of history..."

"...sitting on their backsides while the soldiers did the fighting," Jude interrupted, sarcastically. "They must have been well-scared playing code games in this posh place, miles away from the enemy."

Tyrone and Big Ben sniggered, while Mrs Beaman gave Jude one of her narrow-eyed stares.

“And this room honours some of our heroines,” said the guide, ignoring Jude and pointing at a row of stiff-haired young women in photos.

I stepped forward to take a closer look. The women in the photos stared back, their faces steely and determined. One of them caught my eye – something about the tilt of her head, the glint in her eyes - it felt familiar. Then I saw it: a necklace of wooden beads, identical to the one Mary still wore around her neck.

"Mary!" I blurted out, the word bursting from my mouth before I could stop it.

“Billy’s found his girlfriend,” sneered Jude. “Like them in their nineties, do you?”

Ignoring him, I examined the picture, but Jude moved between me and Mary’s photo, puckering his mouth and making kissing sounds.

“Get lost, Jude,” I said, pushing him out of the way.

Jude’s punch in the stomach took me by surprise and, doubling up in pain, I knocked the clipboard out of the hands of the tour guide.

“That’s it, Jude Doyle,” snapped Mrs Beaman. “You can go and wait in the bus until the tour’s over.”

By the time we piled back in the coach at the end of the visit, Jude was fuming, having spent two phoneless hours alone with the driver. I went to sit at the back with Elliot, trying to ignore the knot of dread which was tightening in my stomach. Jude wouldn't let this go. If he found out I lived at Autumn Days he'd have a field day, telling everyone at school. There'd be no escaping it.

Back at school, darkness and rain were setting in, but I turned left out of the gates instead of right. I couldn't take any chances.

Almost immediately, a low voice murmured, "We're right behind you."

Jude.

I quickened my pace, pulling up the hood of my coat against the hammering rain.

"We're coming for you, Billy Loser," squeaked Big Ben's high-pitched voice.

"Getting closer, you ain't got no chance," growled Tyrone's low one.

I turned to face them and Jude stopped, planting his feet. He ran his hands through his spiky blond mop of hair and sniffed, threateningly. Big Ben was standing behind, towering over Jude, a glob of dribble hanging from his mouth, glistening in the streetlights.

"Go on then," I said, folding my arms as though I couldn't care less. "What've you and your miniscule brains decided to do to me?

"You ready to face it, Ember?" said Jude, taking another step towards me. "Ain't no way you're getting outta this one."

I turned back to find Tyrone in front of me, blocking my path, his black puffer jacket making him even wider than usual.

Trapped between them, I had nowhere to go. The prickly hedge to my left was too thick; the busy road was my only option. I had to take a split-second decision.

With the rain lashing in my face, and the roar of traffic pounding in my ears, all rational thought was drowned out and I stepped into the road thinking the gap between the cars was wide enough.

Too late, I saw I wasn't going to make it to the other side. The gap vanished, headlights blinded me and the grill of a monstrous lorry loomed into view, its horn resounding in my head. I squeezed my eyes shut, waiting for the impact...

... a strong grip yanked me back onto the pavement and into the prickly hedge. Through the thorns, I could just make out the back of a black hoodie. The wearer was shouting at Jude whose face had gone into reverse. Big Ben's slobber was bouncing up and down like a slimy yo-yo and Tyrone was staring at the ground. The three of them shot off in the opposite direction, leaving me to identify Black Hoodie, but a pair of trousers blocked my view.

"What d'you think you're doing, idiot? You were this close to being run over! Are you okay?" said the man, pulling me out of the hedge and eyeing the queue of traffic building up.

"Yeah, I'm okay. Sorry, I tripped," I said.

The man shook his head and returned to his lorry, "Watch where you're going next time."

I stood for a moment, puzzling over the identity of Black Hoodie. What had he said to make Jude run away like that?

I needed to get home quickly, before Neelam started to worry. My heart was still thumping from the chase, but at least Jude hadn't been able to follow me.

I couldn't let him find out I lived on the dementia floor of a care home.

Two

Russia, six-and-a-half years ago

Manya stood in the garden, knocking the heads off purple irises with a stick.

"I don't want to go all the way to Moscow," she muttered, choosing two new victims. "And I don't want to go to Pushkin." She stamped the purple flowers into the grass to emphasise the point.

"We will be leaving in precisely three minutes and forty-two seconds," her father's irritated voice resounded from the house. "And you had better be ready, young lady."

Strains of Beethoven wafted through an upstairs window and Manya could see the back of her mother's head. It was always the back of her head because Mrs Molchalin looked away whenever her daughter came into view.

Manya reluctantly made her way inside. She would try one last attempt to persuade her grandmother to come on the long trip.

"Please, Babushka," she begged. "You'd enjoy a day out, and maybe you could tell me stories on the way, and...and..." she lowered her voice. "...and I need you to come. How can I decide without you?"

Babushka glanced up at Mr Molchalin, who was glowering down at her, and she shook her head.

"Not this time Manya," she said. "This is a special day for you and your papa. Tell me all about it when you get home. You will..."

"...that's it, we're leaving right now," interrupted Mr Molchalin. "What will they think of us if we're late? It's a huge honour to have been invited today and we need to make the right impression."

Manya sulkily climbed into the car next to her father. She knew how ambitious he was for his only daughter, but he pushed too hard. If she went to the distinguished Pushkin Academy, he would put even more pressure on her.

She had only been to Moscow once before. A few years earlier, Babushka had taken her on the train to see Red Square. It had been the best day of her life and Manya remembered every detail. They had visited St Basil's Cathedral with its colourful, swirling towers. They'd paid their respects to Russia's great leader, Vladimir Lenin, at his mausoleum, and they'd ended the day overwhelmed by the beauty of Swan Lake, danced at the Bolshoi Theatre. Manya's most vivid memory was of the Tsar Bell, the largest bell in the whole world. It had been broken during a fire in the Kremlin and never been rung.

"Take a good look at that bell, Manya." Babushka had said. "Magnificent, yet completely useless. Don't become like the

Tsar's bell." At home, her grandmother had given Manya a tiny replica of the bell to remind her of their day together.

Her father's voice interrupted Manya's memories. "You do know I've taken a day off work to accompany you today!" he said, angrily.

Manya remained silent. Her father rarely took time off work, even for holidays. He was proud of the engineering business he had built up himself, and she knew how much he wanted her to join him when she was older. But Manya had no intention of joining DM Engineering. She would find her own career and earn enough money to buy a house, where she and Babushka would live together, away from her parents.

"You could show a bit more enthusiasm," he continued. "It's the most prestigious school in Moscow. Did I tell you about the brand-new athletics track?"

"Yes, you did," said Manya, wondering how Papa could possibly think a running track would appeal to her.

"And they have an interactive sandbox where you can learn about rivers and volcanoes."

"Cool," she said, equally unimpressed.

"You'll make new friends," he persisted. "Friends who might come closer to matching your intelligence."

Friends were the last thing Manya wanted. She'd had a friend once and it was a painful memory. Manya never knew why Svetlana had sought her out, but the girl had flattered her, brought sweets to school for her, and sat next to her every lunchtime.

For her eighth birthday, Babushka had encouraged Manya to invite Svetlana for tea. They'd spent the whole morning preparing for the guest, baking little cakes and cookies, cutting tiny sandwiches and squeezing fresh oranges and lemons. Mrs Molchalin had turned off the ever-present German symphonies and gone out for the day, taking with her the cold tension which permeated the house whenever she was present. Babushka put on some modern music and danced with Manya until her legs became too tired.

"This is how a birthday should be," she said.

Svetlana arrived with a glorious present for Manya: a set of silver-coloured jewellery embellished with plastic diamonds and rubies. Manya was ecstatic when Babushka helped her put on the necklace, ring and clip-on earrings and Svetlana laughed, clapped her hands and told Manya she looked like a princess.

Mrs Molchalin arrived home unexpectedly. She stopped the music, ripped off Manya's necklace and earrings, and stormed out of the house again announcing that she would return in ten minutes.

"And there are to be no children here when I get back!" she added.

Manya was mortified.

Babushka tried to persuade Svetlana to stay, but the girl was terrified and asked Babushka to take her home. Manya fled to her room and stayed there for the rest of the evening, twisting the ring, the sole surviving piece of jewellery, round and round her finger.

Svetlana decided not to be friends with Manya anymore, and Manya, never wanting to face such humiliation again, began to build a wall of protection around herself by avoiding the other children. She became more and more studious, and this pleased her father enormously. He was thrilled when she started coming top in her class, and almost delirious when, at the age of eleven, the head teacher wrote to tell him Manya had been invited for a preliminary tour of Pushkin Academy, the school for Russia's most gifted and talented pupils.

The journey from Smolensk took four hours, and it was a relief to Manya when they finally arrived. They were greeted by one of the older students who guided them to the large modern entrance hall with its flat panel display screens, each showing a different part of the school.

Lunch had been laid out near the entrance for the prospective pupils and their parents. Tables were laden with cold lamb kebabs, black rye bread, stuffed peppers and colourful salads. Manya tried not to make eye contact with any of the other children, although she couldn't help glancing up at the screens every now and then. She had never imagined a school with so many bright classrooms and such beautiful grounds.

The pupils and their parents were separated and put into small groups for tours of the school. Manya found herself being led into one of the study-bedrooms.

"Each student has their own room where they can study without being disturbed," said the teacher showing them round.

Manya hardly noticed the tastefully decorated room, she was more interested in the laptop on the desk. The teacher explained that all the pupils at Pushkin were given a new laptop on arrival. "We are grateful for the government sponsorship," she added.

The tour continued, and Manya admired the neat classrooms with colourful desks, interactive boards and large windows looking out onto vast green lawns.

"This is the music department," said the teacher. "Our latest addition is software to create special sound effects and music for films." She flicked a few switches and a montage of animal videos appeared on a large screen. "Would any of you like to make some music to accompany the animals?"

Nobody volunteered and Manya kept her head down, she wasn't interested in music. Eventually, a boy with dark curly hair tentatively raised his hand.

"I'd like to have a go please," he said.

He sat down at the keyboard and put on headphones, stretched out his fingers and looked up at the screen where some monkeys were playing in a tree. Suddenly, they were accompanied by a light, bouncy rhythm. Elephants appeared and the music changed to regal marching. Finally, a pair of swans took off from a lake and the music soared with them. The film ended and the boy reluctantly took off the headphones. The teacher nodded appreciatively and Manya stared in awe at the boy who must surely have secured his place at the school.

"This is our ICT suite," said the teacher as they proceeded into a large room filled with state-of-the-art computer screens with keyboards to match. Manya caught her breath, it was like stepping into a space-age control room.

Manya waited hopefully for the teacher to ask if anyone would like to try out the computers, happy to volunteer in this room, but the teacher continued her explanation.

"Our technology is completely up to date. These 3-D printers have already created various intricate parts for new machines. Our coding programme is the most sophisticated in Russia, compiled by students from the Moscow State University itself."

This was where Manya belonged. Her current school had introduced ICT as a new subject two years earlier and Mr Stepanov, the teacher, had enthusiastically organised an after-school computer club. Manya had signed up and become instantly mesmerised by the intricacies of coding. However, when her father discovered she had only come third in a Russian language test he had been furious.

"What's this?" he'd shouted, "Third? You only came third? Manya, how are you to make the name Molchalin great if you don't come top in every subject? You've let me down badly. From now on you will come home straight after school to study our beautiful language."

"But I'm working on a computer project after school!" Manya protested.

"Did you hear me?" he bellowed. "Straight home after school."

Well, Papa, thought Manya, *If I come to this school, you won't be able to stop me going to the ICT Suite! You won't even know!* And she smiled to herself.

The head teacher was waiting for them back in the entrance hall with a rousing speech.

"If you're accepted at Pushkin, you will enjoy plenty of benefits, but you will also be expected to work hard and reach your potential. Today has been a taste of what you can look forward to if you pass the Pushkin entrance exam. The fact that you're here means you have reached, no, surpassed the level of expectation at your current school. You're just one step away from admission to this marvellous academy."

The teacher spoke in a way that filled them all with pride. Manya could feel the determination in the air. Every child in the room would be working hard to pass the exams. Every child wanted to be accepted at Pushkin.

Three

England, the present

It was dark and wet, and my heart was still thumping.

I stumbled through the car park, squinting up at the massive building where the words "Autumn Days Care Home" were etched into a granite slab. Pushing open the glass front door, warm air hit me, along with the familiar smell of washing powder and Elvis Presley telling me I wasn't "nothin' but a hound dog".

I put on a smile and waved at the residents who were enjoying their ritual of afternoon tea and cake before running up the stairs to the dementia floor.

Everyone was asleep, including Mary, but I couldn't wait to tell her what I'd seen.

"Mary," I said, pulling up a chair and holding her wrinkled hand. "I never knew you were a code-breaker! I went on a school trip to Bletchley Park today, and I saw your photo."

Mary looked at me, confused.

"You worked at Bletchley during the war, didn't you?" I said, slowly and clearly.

Mary's eyes opened wide and she put a finger up to her lips as though it was still a big secret. "Cass tor coss libe," she said.

"That's what the tour guide told us," I said. "Careless talk costs lives. But Mary, the war is over now, and it's okay for people to know you worked there. It's really cool, actually and I knew it was you for sure because you were wearing those beads."

Mary's hands clasped the beads which were almost the same as in the photo. The only difference was the random pattern. It looked like a child had restrung the beads for her, all in the wrong order. She looked anxiously over at Frank, but he was asleep.

I didn't want to upset her, so I put the tray with her colouring book on her lap and went to see Gran who'd woken up.

"Who's my flying baby then? Wheeee!" she was saying to her doll, Dardar.

"Hi Gran, I'm here!" I said.

"I've just got back from flip flap," said Gran. "Ooh it was so lovely, and there were ever so many pingle woodles. No zingzong for my elephant on the shoeshine!"

I tried to concentrate as Gran told me all about her day, flying to the moon to buy flowers, but my mind kept wandering back to the close shave with Jude and how terrible it would be if he ever found out I lived at Autumn Days.

Zoning back to the present, Gran was talking about planting petunias in welly boots, and Beryl hobbled over to see what was going on.

"Have you got a girlfriend yet?" she asked, like she does every day. Then she laughed at her joke, like she does every day, and said, "Don't make me laugh, I'll get wrinkles!"

I like Beryl, but she's very nosy, incredibly embarrassing, and she's got no filter. At the weekend, I'd spent nearly an hour helping her to pick up a thousand pieces of jigsaw. I know it was a thousand because it said on the box, alongside the picture of a bodybuilder with bulging biceps.

"Where'd you get this from?" I'd asked.

"Bought it online," Beryl had said, proudly. "By myself. Where d'you think I got your calendar, eh? Bought that online too."

Beryl had given me a Spurs calendar for my birthday, and I'd hung it on my bedroom wall next to the "To Dare Is To Do" sticker. She bought six calendars, all the same, and gave one to me. She kept the other five and hung them in her room, all open on different months. When I first saw them I thought I had a fellow supporter, but I reckon she just likes looking at the players.

Frank marched over with his interrogation face.

"Billy you were late, where've you been?"

Frank's ninety-five and smart.

"Been on a school trip," I said. "The coach got back late." Lying to Frank isn't a good idea because he always notices. I reckon he has a built-in lie-detector left over from his army training.

"Coach full of prickly bushes was it? Is that how you got all them scratches on yer face and leaves all over yer back?"

I wasn't going to tell Frank about Jude. I wasn't ready to talk about it yet. Luckily Mandy came over with a tray of what she calls her 'lemon dribble cake'. I grabbed the biggest slice and scarpered to my room, while Frank worked out which was the next biggest piece.

I needed space to think about what had happened at school and, knowing Jude, once he'd chosen a victim he wouldn't let go. Apart from facing physical annihilation, my main problem was not to let him find out I lived on the dementia floor of an old people's home because he'd tell everyone. Then people would ask why. What could I say?

I finished the cake and looked outside.

Last week Jude's victim was Dylan. On Monday, Dylan's coat was flushed down the toilet, on Tuesday, the sole of Dylan's shoe was ripped off between two clamps in the physics lab. On Friday, Dylan was taken to hospital with a suspected broken nose. With Dylan out of the way, Jude would be looking for someone else to pick on.

I was still looking out of my bedroom window, trying to guess Jude's next move, when Neelam put her head round the door.

"Ah Billy, you're back. How was Bletchley?"

"Good. And guess whose photo I saw hanging on the wall," I said.

Neelam didn't have a chance to guess because one of the carers put her head round the door. "Neelam, could you come please?" she said. "Beryl's making a fuss about sitting in the chair with the owl cushions or something."

"Sorry, Billy," said Neelam. "Tell me later."

I quietly shut the door behind Neelam and sat down at my desk with a sheet of paper and wrote 'Investigation' at the top of the page. Bletchley had inspired me to revisit my own mystery. For so many years I'd accepted that 'the authorities' were looking for my parents, but suddenly, I knew it couldn't be true, someone was lying, intentionally lying. It was time to begin my own investigation.

It wouldn't be my first investigation, but it would be my last because this time I wouldn't give up until I'd found Mum and Dad. For as long as I could remember, I'd been waiting for my parents to come back and, over the years, I'd spent hours trying to work out what happened. I'd interrogated Gran hundreds of times, but she can't even remember her own name. Even *my* name isn't completely real. Louis called me Billy Ember. Billy because that was the name on my pyjamas the night of the fire, and Ember because I was what was left after the fire. I like it.

Louis is the firefighter who rescued me and Gran. He comes to visit and sometimes we play football in the park. He takes me on trips too, and I had a good idea about where I wanted to go for our next trip – the scene of the crime. The place where I lived with Mum, Dad and Gran before someone set fire to our house.

Four

Russia, six years ago

"And the special award for highest academic achievement goes to Manya Molchalin," said the head teacher. Manya made her way to the podium in the Great Hall, listening to the applause and wishing she was somewhere else.

The other students were sitting up straight in their chairs, clapping dutifully, little grimaces on their faces. Manya had won the school's most prestigious prize and they were struggling not to reveal their contempt.

Manya wasn't interested in the other pupils and didn't care what they thought or whether they were jealous. She looked over to the only person who was genuinely pleased about her prize: her father. Mr Molchalin was ecstatic. He had always known Manya would do well, but she had surpassed all expectations, paving the way to his ultimate goal, which was to make the name Molchalin great. He glanced over at his wife with her stony face, barely concealing that ever-present, unforgiving expression and sighed. He would not let her ruin this moment. He looked back at his daughter.

Manya's gaze had switched from her father to her mother. Mrs Molchalin was wearing her smart grey suit with the fox-fur collar, her black hair scraped back tightly, her red lipstick glistening against her pale skin. She wasn't looking at her daughter and Manya was astonished that she'd even come to the ceremony. She remembered Babushka's words.

"Manya, there is nothing you can do about it, your mother will never forgive you. You need to be strong. You can do anything you set your mind to, I will always be proud of you."

Thinking about Babushka brought tears to Manya's eyes, and she looked down.

I will not show emotion. I am strong. I can do anything, she silently chanted.

The prize had guaranteed her place at Pushkin, and she was glad to be going. Life would be unbearable at home without Babushka, there was nothing for her in Smolensk. She raised her eyes again to the sea of faces, sour and unfriendly. She didn't need any of them.

It was the custom for parents to take their children for afternoon tea in the nearby town after the prize-giving ceremony. Manya had begged her father not to go, but he had insisted.

"Why not?" he'd asked, "I have the cleverest, most accomplished daughter in the whole school, and I want to show her off. I want everyone to see that I, Dmitri Molchalin, am the father of a child prodigy. You never know who might be taking tea at the next table. There are some very influential families at your school, Manya. We mustn't miss any opportunities."

So Manya found herself sitting between her parents in the most expensive tearoom in Smolensk. A three-tiered cake tray sat on the table in front of her, heaving with stuffed eggs, honey cakes and tiny Charlotte apple pies. Manya couldn't eat, she sat with her hands folded together on the navy skirt of her neatly pressed uniform. Her tight blazer was too hot, but her father would not allow her to remove it. He too was clearly struggling in his thick dark suit. Beads of sweat were forming at the top of his forehead, and his neck was reddening above the white starched collar of his shirt. Mr Molchalin was systematically working his way around the cake tray and Manya wondered how there was room for the great gulps of food to fit past his tightly bound throat.

Her mother was wearing her absent expression and remained silent throughout. Her father spoke constantly.

"Manya, I have told you before that my investment in your education has always been about the contacts. If you look over there you will see Mr Kozlov – he practically runs Russian Railways. Is his daughter in your class?"

Manya remained silent. She didn't look over to the Kozlov table. Alena had tried to befriend Manya last year, but Manya didn't want to be friends with anyone after the disaster with Svetlana. So she had told Alena she had a highly contagious skin condition, and it would be better for Alena to keep her distance. It had worked.

"And what about Dr Orlov? Do you know his daughter?"

Manya shook her head. Polina Orlov had once tried to copy Manya's work during a test, and when she realised, Manya had produced a dramatic yawn. She'd stretched her arms widely, and strategically tipped a bottle of water over Polina's work.

"Whoa, Polina," Manya had cried. "I didn't see that bottle right next to your paper. Maybe you should move further away." Manya had gone back to her test as Polina tried to salvage what was left of her dripping paper.

The tearoom hummed with low voices and tinkling teacups. Her father's voice broke in once more.

"So, Manya Molchalin," he said, loudly enough for everyone in the tearoom to hear. "Now that you've won the top prize, you will move to Pushkin Academy, the school for the gifted and talented. A year early," he added, his voice increasing in volume. Manya cringed and looked at the floor. Some of the other families turned briefly to look at the Molchalins. None of them smiled.

Manya sat on her bed with a framed photo of her grandmother.

"I wish you could still be here, Babushka," Manya whispered to the photo. "What would you have said about my new school?

Would you have been excited for me, or would you have missed your Myshka, your little mouse?"

A few weeks before the awards ceremony, Babushka had suddenly become very ill. Manya sat next to her grandmother's rocking chair, talking to her, reading to her, or just holding her hand.

One morning, as they were sitting in silence, with the sun streaming through the window, Babushka suddenly let out a sob. Manya was afraid and asked if her grandmother needed a drink. Babushka had taken the emerald ring off her wizened finger and clasped Manya's tight fists between her own gnarled hands.

"You need to take this ring," she wheezed. "It belonged to my father."

"Ivan," whispered Manya. "I know you were close to him."

Babushka's eyes clouded over with her memories. "He was a very special man with so much to give," she said. "I see him in you, Manya. He believed in justice, equality, and peace and he was going to change the world. The day he left for the last time, he pressed this ring into my hand, asking me to keep it safe until he returned."

"Returned from where?"

"He never returned," said Babushka, shaking her head sadly. "They stopped him before he had a chance to make a difference. But maybe *you* will make a difference, my little Myshka, and you will wear his ring. See, his name is engraved on the inside of the gold band. When you wear it, remember me, remember Ivan."

"No, Babushka..." protested Manya, but the old lady shook her head to silence her. Manya slipped off her old plastic ring, the one Svetlana had given her, and replaced it with the green emerald.

Babushka nodded her head in approval and continued.

"Manya, I have to tell you about your mama. I should have told you years ago, but I could never find the words. I should have seen something was wrong with her when she was a child. As her mama, I should have done something before it was too late. Now I can only ask for your forgiveness."

Manya's fear intensified. Babushka's breathing was shallow and gasping, but she didn't call her father, she wanted to hear the story.

"What should you have told me, Babushka? Whatever it is, I forgive you, please tell me," begged Manya.

Babushka's watery blue eyes fixed on the arm of the rocking chair, as she began.

"When Inga, your mama, was a child, she played with dolls. She had twelve dolls and looked after them as though they were real children. Six boys and six girls. They all had names, their own clothes, birthdays, habits and characters. Inga took them everywhere with her. She fed them, bathed them and put them to bed every evening. To begin with, I thought it was a sweet game for a girl to play and I encouraged it. I made more clothes for the dolls, and I even bought her a big pram so she could push them around.

"But Babushka," interrupted Manya, "that sounds normal. Lots of little girls play with dolls."

"That's what I thought," replied her grandmother. "However, it was the beginning of an obsession that got out of control.

"One day, when she was about your age, she told me she was 'preparing for the real thing'. That she was going to have twelve children of her own."

"Did she really want twelve children?" asked Manya, incredulously. She had always believed her mother didn't even *like* children.

"Oh yes," answered Babushka, sadly. "The Motherland is very proud of women who have lots of children; it's seen as a wonderful achievement. At fifteen, Inga was still caring for her dolls as though they were real children. It didn't surprise me when she married your father at twenty and was expecting her first child before her twenty-first birthday. She was convinced she was having a boy because her eldest doll had been a boy named Ivan, after her grandfather.

"There were complications during the birth. At one point, Inga and the baby were both in danger, but the doctors and midwives miraculously saved them."

"Was that me?" asked Manya, tremulously. She had never been told about her birth and had no idea she'd been ill.

"Yes, Manya, you were that baby. You were both very sick and had to stay in hospital for a long time. Your father sat by Inga's bedside almost every day, and I would sit with you, my poor little Myshka. Finally, you were both well enough to go home, but Inga didn't want to take you because you were a girl. She wanted a boy."

Babushka looked at her granddaughter with tears in her eyes. She was reliving a nightmare that had been buried in the back of her memory for a long time. Manya couldn't speak. She was holding her breath, and all she could manage was a small nod of her head. Why hadn't Babushka or her father told her before? All these years of hurt and rejection, just because she was a girl? A deep fury began to well up in Manya and her eyes blazed.

But Babushka hadn't quite finished.

"Your father brought you home, of course, and we looked after you together. Eventually he had to explain to Inga that she would not be able to have any more children, and she broke down completely. It was as if her whole life had been ruined and she blamed you, her daughter. She only ever gave you one thing Manya: your name.

Half an hour later, Manya found her mother's dictionary of baby names hidden in a shelf behind some recipe books. Leafing through the book, her heart thumped as she looked for the right page and ran her finger down the columns until she found what she was looking for. Manya stared at the book for a moment, allowing tears to well up and blur the words. Then she ran from the room, slamming the door behind her. The book lay on the floor, broken and torn. Part of one page remained defiantly upturned, revealing the meaning of the name Manya: sea of bitterness.

Five

England, the present

Ever since I can remember, Louis has gone along with my ideas for finding my parents. When I was very small, I was convinced they'd been captured by pirates, and Louis took me to the beach with a pair of binoculars. We spent the day looking out for ships flying the Jolly Roger flag, but we only saw container ships, sailing boats and a man on a paddle board. I don't remember being disappointed, but I do remember eating three ice-creams.

When I was a bit older, I decided my parents must have been abducted by aliens. Louis found an observatory for me to look for flying saucers through a big telescope. I didn't see any aliens, but there were plenty of cool stars to look at.

So when I asked him to take me to where my house had been, I knew he'd do it.

"I'm not quite sure this is going to help, so don't get your hopes up," he said in the car. "It used to be a quiet little village with just a few houses, but soon after the fire, some builder bought the land and turned it into a big housing estate."

"Did he put a new house up where mine used to be?"

"Probably. I haven't been back for years. I'm not even sure I can remember the exact location."

I tried to imagine myself as one of those spies in the films the Oldies watch endlessly. I know most of them off by heart because they like playing the same ones over and over. They can't remember what film they saw the day before, so it doesn't matter if it's always 'The 39 Steps' or 'Our Man in Havana'. Every time 'North By Northwest' comes on, Beryl says, "Ooh, I love this film, I saw it at the pictures." (Oldie speak for cinema). "That Cary Grant, he was such a dish!" (Oldie speak for good-looking).

As we got closer I began to feel panicky. How would it feel to visit the place where my parents had been kidnapped, and where I'd nearly died in a fire? I shouldn't have worried though because when we got there, all I could see was a bunch of boring houses looking the same as each other. Louis parked the car, and we started walking up and down the roads. They had very similar names: Doyle Close, Doyle Avenue, Doyle Way.

"Why are so many roads called Doyle?" I asked Louis.

"I don't know," he said. "Maybe the builder's name was Doyle."

It was my next clue: Jude's surname is Doyle. If his dad was involved with the estate, he might have known my parents. He might even have spoken to them before the fire.

On my way to school the next morning, I thought about Jude and tried to figure out how I was going to talk to his dad. Jude was a bully, that was certain. The rumour was that he'd been expelled from his last school.

Big Ben and Tyrone were at my junior school, and although I'd never been friends with them, they used to be harmless. Big and a bit stupid, they would clump about as a pair, and the worst they would do would be to bump into someone on purpose and run off giggling together. But since Jude came to school in September, it was as though he was the leader they'd been waiting for. Tyrone followed Jude, and slobbery Big Ben followed Tyrone, usually with his mouth full of something and dribbling a lot of it down his front.

I'd just sat down when Katie, a girl in my class, approached my desk as though she was about to tell me something urgent, but Mrs Beaman came in.

"Katie, what are you doing out of your seat?" she said. "Sit down, stop talking and get out your books."

Big Ben was sniggering.

"Benjamin Brown that includes you," said Mrs Beaman. "And put the fish fingers away. You shouldn't eat them straight out of the packet, they'll make you ill."

I didn't know why Katie wanted to talk to me. She was the other new person in our class, and I'd never spoken to her before. I waited until break, thinking she might find me, but I didn't see her, I saw Jude.

"We've got a treat for you today, Billy," he said, jabbing a finger at me, threateningly. Big Ben tried to do the same but managed to poke himself in the eye. It would have been funny, but after their last attempt to corner me, I couldn't help wondering what Jude and his gang had in store for me.

At lunch, I managed to get near the front of the queue. Jude and Tyrone appeared right behind, nudging each other and pressing up close to me.

"You're dead, Ember," said Jude.

"You've got it coming," growled Tyrone.

Slobbery Big Ben, the third member of Jude's gang, had already got his lunch. He closed in on me, trying to balance the enormous pile of food he'd just loaded onto a plate.

"Gonna getcha, gork!" he spat, slobber bursting from his vast mouth and dropping at least four sausages off his tray. He bent down to pick them up and managed to tip the whole plate onto the floor. He didn't seem to care; he just scooped it all up and licked his hands.

I got my food and was about to look for a table when Katie came to stand next to me with her tray.

"Come and sit over here and start eating," she whispered, dramatically.

We sat down.

"Listen," said Katie. "I was walking behind the idiots this morning on my way to school and I heard what they were saying. I wanted to tell you earlier, but I didn't get the chance."

"So what did they say?" I asked.

"They've got this really stupid idea that they're going to sit with you for lunch."

"That doesn't sound too bad," I said.

"Look," said Katie, "I'm just trying to help. They have this gross idea about distracting you so you look away from your food, and while you're looking away, they're all going to spit on your plate. I'm telling you so you *don't* look away. Keep looking at your food. Okay, they're coming, I'll stay here."

I didn't want three globs of spit on my plate, so I stayed where I was and kept eating.

"Ahh, that's sweet," said Jude. "Billy's got himself a new girlfriend."

I ignored him, so did Katie.

Suddenly Jude pointed to the table behind me and shouted, "Look! Mrs Cannon's dyed her hair."

I was about to turn to look at Mrs Cannon's dyed hair when Katie kicked me. Tyrone had already leaned forward, and his mouth was dangerously close to my plate.

"Her hair, it's bright orange!" persisted Jude.

"Grow up Jude," said Katie.

I carried on eating, but glanced up to see what slobbery Big Ben and Tyrone were doing on the opposite side of the table. Big Ben's cheeks were bulging and there was dribble running down from one side of his mouth.

I could feel Katie shaking beside me. Was she scared? I looked at her, she was laughing! Jude angrily shoved the bench back and stood up.

"C'mon!" he snarled at Big Ben and Tyrone. "We don't want to sit with these two doughnuts, they're putting me off my food."

"Where are the doughnuts?" I heard Big Ben asking Jude.

And that was the beginning of my friendship with Katie.

Six

Russia, six years ago

Babushka died before the awards ceremony.

At the funeral, Manya stole a glance at her mother. Mrs Molchalin might have been sad, but if she was, she kept it well hidden. The expression on her blank face never changed. It made Manya feel angry, until she considered her own features. Her eyes were not filled with tears, and her mouth was probably fixed in the same straight line. She shook her head in alarm to think she might resemble her mother in any way.

Manya was devastated. Her grandmother had been the only person who had ever really loved her. Her father appreciated her achievements, but Manya was aware that his pride was for her success, not for her. He had confirmed this in the tearoom after the ceremony when he seemed more concerned about impressing the other parents. He was delighted that Manya had been accepted at Pushkin, but not for her sake. It was for him; he couldn't wait to show off.

Manya began at the new school soon after her twelfth birthday. Mrs Molchalin had neither celebrated the birthday, nor had she acknowledged the fact that her only child was going away to boarding school. Mr Molchalin drove her in his old Lada. He'd acquired the new uniform and the books she needed, and left Manya to pack her belongings alone. She briefly considered how the Molchalin house would feel with just her parents in it, but only briefly. She was more concerned with how her own life would change.

When they arrived at school, Mr Molchalin helped Manya with her bags. An older girl showed them to Manya's room, but immediately left them alone. They stood awkwardly for a moment, then Mr Molchalin put one hand on Manya's shoulder and said, "I want you to do your very best here, Manya. You will make the name 'Molchalin' great."

And without another word, he left the room, shutting the door behind him.

Manya sat on the bed, looking at the bags in a heap on the floor.

There was a knock on the door which made her jump, and she stood up quickly. The boy with the dark, curly hair, the one who had played music so beautifully during the Pushkin tour, stood at the door. He was dressed in the Pushkin uniform of navy suit, white shirt and bright red tie. A silver crucifix peeped out from between the buttons. Manya wondered why he'd already changed into his uniform. Lessons didn't begin until Monday.

"Hi, I'm Feliks. I'm in the room next door."

Manya waited for him to continue, but after his bold introduction he seemed to falter. She hadn't thought about the other pupils at all and hadn't intended to get to know anybody. She'd come here to study. But here was this boy looking eagerly at her, and she found herself speaking.

"I'm Manya. Did you get in because you're good at music?"

Feliks looked a little taken aback and Manya realised she might have chosen her words more carefully.

"I s'pose," he said. "Yeah, that's probably how I got my place here. But I don't really play an instrument, I compose. I use technology."

Technology was a word that appealed to Manya.

"What do you mean, you use technology to compose?"

"I'll show you if you like," said Feliks, and he beckoned for her to follow him to his room next door.

Feliks must have arrived a while ago because he'd already unpacked his belongings. An alarm clock stood on the table next to his bed, folders sat on his desk and photos had been stuck on his wall.

"Is that your family?" she asked.

"Yes. I've got three sisters and a brother."

"Five children?" gaped Manya. "Was your mum pleased to get rid of one?" She regretted her words when she saw Feliks's sad expression.

"No," he said simply. "She cried a lot. She didn't want me to come here."

Manya needed to change the subject. The last thing she wanted to discuss was parents. Particularly mothers.

"Let's hear this music then," she said.

"I've just uploaded some of my pieces," said Feliks. "Listen."

He clicked a few buttons on the laptop on his desk and a dark grey sea popped up. Quiet music was playing in the background which seemed to pulse in time with the waves. Manya was about to speak when the music changed tempo and became more dramatic, perfectly synchronised with the altered rhythm of the angry sea.

"I composed this last year," said Feliks. "I can't wait to use the computers here. They have these special programmes which can synchronise the sound and pictures more accurately. So what's your special subject?" he asked.

Manya thought for a moment. For the first time in her life she considered her words. In the past she would have come back with a quick, "None of your business," but for some reason she felt as though she could share something with Feliks.

"I'm not bad at maths, but I really love computer programming."

Suddenly, a loud bell sounded in the corridor, followed by a voice shouting, "Dinner time. Everybody to the dining-room."

"Let's go," said Manya, looking at Feliks in his uniform and then at her own jeans and t-shirt. "But why don't you change out of your uniform. It'll be really embarrassing if you're the only one wearing it. I'll wait in my room."

"But I thought…." Manya didn't hear the rest, she had already shut the door.

Five minutes later, Manya and Feliks opened the massive oak door that led into the dining-room. Usually when pupils entered this vast room for the first time, they noticed the carved wooden panelling along the walls, the stained-glass windows, the heavy, glass chandeliers or the large marble statue of Alexander Pushkin himself, Russia's greatest poet. But the only thing Manya and Feliks noticed was the fact that all the other children were wearing their school uniforms.

One by one, the other children stopped talking to each other and stared at them. A stern looking woman came over and, without bothering to spare them any humiliation, spoke in a voice that everyone else in the room could hear.

"When you are at Pushkin, you follow the rules. The rules state quite clearly that you are to wear school uniform in the dining-room. You're already late, so go and get your food."

Manya looked apologetically at Feliks. He'd been right about wearing the uniform, and now he would be angry with her.

This is why I don't want friends, she thought to herself miserably. *Something bad happens and then they don't like me anymore.*

They joined the queue to collect their plates of food. Manya was behind a very large girl with long bushy hair tied loosely in a ponytail which kept brushing across Manya's face. She would have liked to move out of the way, but didn't dare turn round. Feliks was right behind her and would think she was getting him into even more trouble. As they approached the serving hatch, the large girl stepped backwards. The force of her immense weight pushed Manya off balance and she felt herself falling. She reached out to hold onto the only support available which unfortunately happened to be the girl's ponytail. As she felt the massive bulk fall on top of her, Manya wondered if this might be the end for her. It would be the shortest time any pupil had lasted at the famous school for the gifted and talented. Finding she had survived the ordeal, she desperately tried to push the girl off, but was completely stuck. Lying entwined on the floor with their arms and legs flailing, the pair had the appearance of some gigantic, upturned beetle.

The hall erupted into laughter. Somehow Manya managed to disentangle herself and stood up. All she could see were pointing fingers and contorted faces. She didn't know whether to lash out or storm out. They were all laughing at her. All except Feliks.

"C'mon Manya, you need to see the funny side. It's worse for her," he said, looking at the other girl who was still thrashing about on the floor.

Later that evening, as Manya got into her new bed in her new room at her new school, she smiled as she reflected upon her first day. It wasn't exactly the start she would have chosen, but it had ended unexpectedly well. Her new friend Feliks hadn't been annoyed that she'd got him into trouble. In fact, after the disastrous dinner, they'd walked back to their rooms together and Feliks had described the scene in the dining-room. He'd made Manya laugh. It was the first time she'd laughed for many, many months.

Seven

England, the present

"Is it true that you worked for a computer company?" I asked Frank after school.

"Who told you that?" asked Frank, looking around the room as though I'd just revealed some top-secret information.

"Neelam. She said you've got a mathematical brain."

"Not sure about a mathematical brain, lad, but I've got some secrets up here," he said, tapping his head. "One of these days I might let you in on my secrets, but not today."

"I forgot to tell you about Mary," I said, hoping to extract Frank's secret surreptitiously. "Did you know she worked at Bletchley Park? I saw her photo there when we were on our school trip."

"Course I know," said Frank. "She's part of the secret."

No matter how much I pushed, Frank wouldn't let me in on his secret, so I decided to tell him about mine. Sharing bad things with him made me feel better because nothing that happened to me could ever be as bad as the things that happened to Frank during the war. He loved to tell me about the sergeant major who was always picking on him:

"I couldn't do anything right for that man. Me boots weren't shiny enough, me hair weren't short enough, me trousers weren't ironed enough. He told me I was so ugly, me face weren't on straight enough! And all the time I would have to answer, 'Yes sir! No sir! Whatever you say sir!' Drove me crackers. He was in charge, and I had to do everything he said."

"Jude isn't in charge," I pointed out.

"In that case just smack him one on the blinkin' nose!" said Frank.

I laughed, but a serious voice behind me broke into our conversation. It was Mandy telling me not to get involved in any smacking.

"It's fine, Mandy, Frank was joking," I said.

Frank pulled a face and picked up his newspaper. He didn't like Mandy, who'd come over with a pile of little pancakes she calls blinis. Mandy works part time as a cook at Autumn Days and she's in the sixth form at school. For some reason, Mandy feels the need to watch out for me which is really annoying and sometimes feels like stalking; popping out all over the place, asking if I'm okay.

Over the past few days she'd been checking up on me even more than usual and I wondered if she'd noticed the friction between me and Jude's gang at school. It didn't surprise me that she'd been listening to my conversation with Frank. I told her I needed to do my homework, just to get away from her.

I went over to where Pascal was sitting in his usual chair by the entrance to Nostalgia. Pascal sits with his eyes shut a lot of the time, pretending to be asleep. But it's easy to tell when he's really asleep because his false teeth rattle when he breathes in. Pascal used to be a ballet dancer in Paris, so he's very useful for French homework. I had a test coming up, and hadn't done any revision.

Pascal's another one who likes listening to other people's conversations. As I sat down next to him, he opened his eyes and looked at me. When Pascal speaks, his eyes flicker very quickly up and down, he stretches out all his fingers and twirls his hands.

"If I know anysing about bullies," said Pascal, in his French accent so it sounded like boolies, "dere's usually somesing going on in de background dat's making zem unhappy. And if somesing's going wrong at home, zey take it out on udder people. Dere was a boy called Etienne at my ballet school. He was good at everysing: arabesques, pliés and pirouettes, but he was mean to everyone. Mais oui, one time he took my shoes and put drawing pins in them! Many years later, he told me his papa used to beat him wis a stick. I bet this boy Shude has a few problems of his own."

...a few problems of his own? My mind started whirring. Yes, that was it! Jude's dad was the problem.

If our house had been in the way of Mr Doyle's new housing estate, he would have tried to persuade my parents to sell it. What if my parents had refused to sell, and Mr Doyle got angry? Was it possible that Jude's dad could have burnt down our house because it was in the way?

That was it! He was so desperate for the house to be out of the way, that in the middle of the night he set fire to it.

He had to make sure my parents were safe, but he also needed to stop them talking. That's when he decided to kidnap them. It all made sense!

"Wow thanks Pasqual," I said. "You've just helped me solve a mystery. Jude's dad kidnapped my parents!"

"Kidnapped your parents? Ooh la la, dis is somesing terrible. You must fight for zem immediatement!"

"That's exactly what I'm going to do," I said.

Eight

Russia, five years ago

Manya had plenty to keep her busy. The work was more difficult than she was used to and, at first, she struggled to keep up. She desperately wanted to get into the ICT suite but there never seemed to be any free time.

Mornings always began with school assembly, where the Head would make an inspiring speech about how the Pushkin pupils were the elite, the best in the country. How, when they had completed their time at school, they would be expected to give something back to the Motherland. Manya didn't understand the speeches to begin with, but over time the head teacher's words began to stick. Every day, as the children filed out of assembly, the Russian National Anthem would be played through the school's sound system. The pupils had to sing as they marched down the corridors to their classrooms. They were supposed to admire the displays on the walls which were covered with pictures of successful Russians and maps of glorious Russia.

Patriotism at Pushkin was extended to all areas of the curriculum. In history Manya learnt about victorious Russian battles, in geography she learnt about the vast extent of the country, and in music, science and language she was taught about brilliant musicians, daring cosmonauts and celebrated authors.

The teachers always expected the best from every student, and Manya found some of them intimidating. Mr Bykov taught General Studies, and was particularly unpredictable.

One morning, the class was finishing the final chorus of the anthem as they entered the classroom. Mr Bykov, an enormous hulk of a man with a Rasputin beard was waiting for them. Manya had learned early on not to talk in class unless invited to do so by the teacher, so she stole a glance at Feliks and pursed her lips.

"Today we are going to learn to think outside the box," said Mr Bykov. "Do you know what that means?"

There was a pause as everyone tried to summon up the courage to answer. Feliks put up his hand, cautiously. "Is it when you have to think about things differently?" he asked, bravely.

"That's right, Feliks. I want you to start thinking creatively, unconventionally, from a new perspective."

Manya gave Feliks a friendly kick of encouragement under the desk. It felt good to have an ally. For the first time in years, Manya felt a connection with another person her own age. She gave him the slightest hint of a thumbs up.

"Let me give you an example," continued Mr Bykov. "What is two plus two?"

Mr Bykov waited, while the children shifted uncomfortably in their seats.

"Come on! What is two plus two?"

Manya desperately wanted to answer but was too afraid. What if the answer wasn't four and Mr Bykov humiliated her? She kept her hands firmly under her knees.

A girl at the other side of the room tentatively put up her hand.

"Is it...erm...is it four?" she asked, timidly.

"Yes of course it's four!" snapped Mr Bykov. "But is two plus two *always* four?" he demanded.

"For example, what if you have two dogs plus two sausages? Then what do you have?"

There was silence. Most heads were down. Nobody wanted to be the one to answer.

"Nobody? Come on! Two dogs plus two sausages? Think outside the box!"

Silence.

"The answer," said Mr Bykov, "is two dogs. Obviously. Think about what happened to the sausages."

The children didn't know whether to laugh. Manya just wished for the lesson to be over.

By the end of the first term, Manya had decided that some of the classes were not worth attending, and discovered how to avoid one lesson altogether. She realised that if her name wasn't on the register, which was taken at the beginning of every lesson, she might not be missed. She quickly selected Russian Language as the first lesson to give up.

I know how to speak my own language, she reasoned, *so why do I need to study it?*

It helped that the language teacher was the oldest, longest serving member of staff. The little old man with thick glasses probably wouldn't even notice she was missing.

"Mr Popov," she ventured one morning, calling his name and putting up her hand at the same time, hoping not to be reprimanded for speaking out of turn. "Would it be possible to shut the blind? The sun is giving me a headache."

Mr Popov shuffled over to the blind and pulled at the string which had stuck. Manya knew it would stick because she had tied a couple of strategic knots in it before the lesson began. It gave her time to walk calmly to the teacher's desk and flick the computer screen to the page with the register. She didn't turn to look at the rest of the class who were staring at her, wide-eyed. Manya scrolled down to her name and deleted it. Manya Molchalin no longer existed in Mr Popov's class.

"Don't expect me in the language classes anymore," she said to Feliks later, on their way back to their rooms.

"Why?"

"I don't need to learn my own language. Just let me know if Mr Popov misses me."

Feliks shrugged and changed the subject. It was one of the good things about him; he didn't ask too many questions.

By the end of her second term at Pushkin, Manya had made a list of other classes to discontinue: art, music, design, religious studies and games. She had worked out that missing these lessons would give her an extra fourteen hours in the ICT suite. She'd also worked out how to skip the lessons without being missed. It had taken a long time to hack into the school's attendance records, but she wasn't going to tell anyone her secret. Not even Feliks.

Manya loved having a laptop in her room, but the computers in the ICT suite were newer and much faster. Now she was able to sit, totally absorbed in front of a screen for hours at a time and made sure to always sit in a corner. She discovered that, if she kept her head down when anyone else came into the room, even if it was a whole class, nobody would question what she was doing there. They would assume she was working on something important and had been given permission.

For Manya, unravelling the mysteries of programming languages and networking protocols was an exciting alternative to lessons and a much more productive way to spend her time, but what had started as inquisitiveness began to take a darker turn. The deeper she delved into the depths of cyberspace, the bolder her ambitions grew. She wanted to improve her skills, not just for the sake of knowledge, but for the thrill of exploration and mastery. She wanted to push the boundaries of what was possible.

Manya's intentions had never been malicious, but her curiosity began to steer into the realm of hacking, infiltrating systems and uncovering secrets. As she sat in front of the computers, her fingers flying across the keys, she felt she was on the brink of unlocking a world of infinite possibilities.

Feliks joined her as often as he could to work on his own projects, and he never asked Manya how she had managed to remove her name from the registers. One evening, he knocked on her door.

"Manya, I don't want to know what you're up to because I don't want to get into trouble myself..."

"Why would *you* get into trouble?" asked Manya.

"If I know what you're doing and the teachers find out, I might be blamed for not telling them," said Feliks.

"It's no big deal," said Manya. "I just don't see the point in some subjects. I'm putting my time to better use."

"But what about the end of year exams? You have to pass all of them, or you won't be invited back to Pushkin," said Feliks.

"Look," said Manya. "It's not your problem. I'm going to pass all the exams. Anyway, I don't know why you're worrying about me when you've got your music competition coming up."

"I just wish I knew what the other entries were going to be," said Feliks. "I haven't got a chance against Nikolai Lenkov. Apparently, he won last year with a score of eighty-nine per cent."

Manya thought for a moment before asking, "Feliks, have you composed any funny music? Something totally ridiculous?"

"Yes, but I'm not entering with that," replied Feliks. "This is supposed to be serious. We have to compose music to go with a video of animals in springtime."

"Hmm, I wouldn't know where to start. But could you send me your funny music?" said Manya, "I just need to borrow it. Don't ask why or I might have to lock you up and throw away the key!"

Two days later, Feliks was in Manya's room again. This time he hadn't knocked.

"How did you get Nikolai's competition entry?" he demanded angrily. "It's on my laptop. It came in an anonymous email with the title, 'Your Wish Come True'. How did it get there?"

Manya looked at Feliks in astonishment. "Why are you so angry? You told me you wished you knew what the other entries were. Now you know Nikolai's."

"But that's cheating, Manya. What did you do? How did you get it? Did he see you in his room?"

"I didn't go to his room."

Feliks shook his head and stormed out.

Manya was confused. Feliks had said he wanted to know what the other entries were, and she had delivered. He was her friend and she'd helped him. Wasn't that what friends did? He must be stressed about the competition, she thought. She would have liked to tell him not to worry, that he would certainly win the competition, but she didn't want to spoil the surprise.

Nine

England, the present

After school the next day, I was disappointed not to find Frank in his usual chair when I got home, and walked towards his room to check he was okay. The door was shut, but I could hear him shouting, "Take me home right now! Get my medals and let me out!"

I took a deep breath and pushed open the door. Baz, one of the carers was trying to get him to sit down, but Frank was standing to attention, his eyes wild as he searched the room for enemies.

"Hiya Frank," I said in my cheeriest voice. "I'm just home from school and I wanted to tell you all about..."

"Keep back, son," barked Frank. "It ain't safe in here. Just walk carefully, atta boy, just like I told you."

"I am walking carefully, but you know Baz. He's one of us. He's on our side."

"Don't let them take me, Billy."

I looked around for something to divert Frank's attention. "Is this your Spitfire?" I asked, slowly taking one of his photos off the wall and holding it out to him.

Frank's eyes flickered away from the imagined threat in the corner, and he glanced down at the photo. "Where'd you get that?" he said.

The spitfire did the trick, and before long Frank was sitting back in his chair, telling me all about his daring expeditions during the war. I was relieved it hadn't taken too long to calm him down. Maybe I'd just got better at understanding.

Frank suddenly decided it was time to go to the lounge for tea, so we went to sit with Mary who lifted her hand in a sort of wave. She was wearing her red dress, the one she used to wear before she had her stroke.

While Frank chatted away to Mary, I thought back to how she used to walk around pretending to be a member of staff. That was before her face went all lopsided and she stopped talking. Poor Mary, she used to be so energetic and friendly, shaking hands with visitors and showing them to a comfortable chair.

"You just wait there," she'd say in her Irish lilt. "I'll go and fetch Jean for you. She took the bus to Dublin about half an hour ago."

The bus – that was it! I could take the bus back to the Doyle Estate.

"Sorry, Mary, Frank," I said. "Just got to go somewhere. Tell Neelam I won't be long."

Getting to places by bus wasn't as easy as I thought. Having found the route, I ran to the nearest bus stop and waited fifteen minutes. I changed twice, and even then had to walk ten minutes to get to Doyle Avenue.

My plan had been to knock on all the doors and ask for Jude. That way I'd find out which was his house. If his Dad was in, I could question him about my parents. It had seemed such a good idea back at home, but after knocking on twenty doors, only five people were in, and none of them seemed thrilled about being disturbed.

Doyle Avenue had ninety-two houses, and when I'd finished there, I still had Doyle Close and Doyle Way stretching far into the distance, with probably another few waste-of-time hundred houses in each of them. If I'd thought more carefully, I'd have realised that this whole area was too far away from school. I knew Jude walked to school; this place wasn't walkable.

Feeling hot and annoyed with myself, I went back to Autumn Days where Frank and Mary were watching a film, so I flopped down in the armchair next to Pasqual.

"I can't believe it, Pasqual. I mean how difficult can it be to find where someone lives?"

"Who are you looking for?" said Pasqual, looking around shiftily. "Maybe I can be of assistance, non?"

"Just my parents," I fumed, trying not to let my frustration bubble over. "Nobody else is bothering to look for them."

"But I know what 'appened to your parents."

"You do?"

"Bah oui. I saw zem peeping in through zat window over there," he said. "It was dark, and I could only make out their silhouettes, but someone was behind zem with a gun. Zey were coming for me!"

"My parents were coming for you?" I asked.

"Ah non! Not your parents. It was Beryl. She was holding a gun and she was pointing it at my het."

"What's a het?" I asked.

"You know a het, it is on top of your neck. Alors, it was very, very dark and Beryl crept in through zat window and tried to pounce on me. She works for the Chinese Government."

I love Pasqual, he knows how to make me smile.

The time had come to tell Katie about my missing parents, but finding the right words could be difficult:

"Hey Katie, come to mine and you can help me find my parents who've been missing for eleven years. Jude's dad kidnapped them."

It didn't sound right.

"Want to meet my family, average age eighty-nine?"

Nope.

Then I imagined taking Katie to Autumn Days. "Katie, this is Beryl. No, Beryl, I'm not going to marry her."

I went back to my search for Jude's dad. Eventually, I found a website which listed thirty-seven Doyles and their landline numbers. This was going to be much easier than walking around knocking on doors.

After sixteen attempts I gave up. Only one person answered, and he hung up on me.

There was only one thing for it. I would have to follow Jude home.

Ten

Russia, Five years ago

Manya was hard at work early on the morning of Feliks's music competition. She had a few adjustments to make and then she wanted to spend some time with him to help calm his nerves.

"I think your entry is fabulous, Feliks," she said, "It was totally brilliant to use that video of the golden eagle chick. I love the bit where the chick's mum is trying to help, and she tips it over the edge of the nest. When it starts to fly the music is amazing!"

"Thanks, but don't you think the crescendo at the end is over-dramatic?" asked Feliks.

"No, it's perfect. Come on, let's go. I want to get a good seat."

The Great Hall was already filling up. This was the music technology students' most important event of the year, and the other children were eager to hear the competition entries.

From her seat in the third row, Manya could quite easily see Feliks and the other competitors who were looking nervous. All except Nikolai who was clearly expecting to win. Feliks had refused to open the attachment in Manya's email which contained Nikolai's competition entry, but Manya had watched it. After all, she had gone to the bother of obtaining it without Nikolai realising, and she was quite proud of herself. She acknowledged Nikolai's was an amazing piece of music accompanying the life cycle of a frog, from spawn to fully grown adult. She still thought Feliks would have had a good chance of winning without her assistance, but she wasn't taking any chances.

The Great Hall became silent as the first girl presented her work. A chestnut horse, galloping through a field of spring flowers, accompanied by a rhythmic melody and the sound of horseshoes. The performance provoked plenty of applause, especially from the girl's friends in the audience. The guest judge was very appreciative and gave a score of eighty. The bar was set high. The next three entries were rather mediocre in both quality and score. Manya lost interest and switched off, until suddenly it was Feliks's turn.

A hush fell as the music began. Manya looked at the smiling faces of the audience as they watched the inquisitive, fluffy eagle chick. Feliks's clever music made the chick look as though he was asking his mum what to do. When the chick finally opened his wings and flew away to a musical crescendo, the hall erupted with applause, and Manya watched Feliks's face change from a tight, pained expression to a big smile of relief. It was over.

The judge was very enthusiastic. "Rarely have I heard such depth of feeling in a composition from someone so young. The precision and intricacy of the music perfectly complementing an inspired choice of film. I congratulate you."

Feliks's score was added to the board: ninety-two per cent.

Manya felt her heart swell with pride for Feliks, but almost immediately alter to a nervous pounding at what was about to happen. She watched as Nikolai arrogantly stepped up to the stage, preparing the computer to show his entry. Manya held her breath as the music began.

Nikolai's self-satisfied expression turned to bewilderment as a fast-paced, catchy beat rose in volume. He turned to look at the screen. Three large frogs were jumping up and down on a wall and puffing out their cheeks as if in time to the comical melody. It was quite a sight. After a stunned silence, the children in the audience burst out laughing and clapping in time to the beat. Some were even stamping their feet. Red-faced, Nikolai rushed to stop the video, but it was too late. He desperately tried to find the correct file, but it was nowhere. Manya knew he wouldn't find it. She had deleted it and inserted the alternative frog video with the goofy music that Feliks had 'lent' her a few days earlier. She looked happily over to Feliks, expecting to see him looking jubilant in victory. His face was not that of a champion, it was livid. He looked at Manya, and his hostile expression felt like a sharp slap. Manya watched in dismay as he ran out of the hall.

"No, I'm not sorry," she insisted later.

"How could you do that to me?" Feliks said. "I thought you were my friend. I really wanted to win that competition and now I'll never know if I could have."

"But you did win."

"No, you cheated!" Feliks was shouting now. "Why did you do it? How did you do it? No, don't tell me. It's wrong, Manya. It's stealing. If this is what you've been working on all these months, you've been wasting your time. I don't think I can ever trust you again. How do I know you're not looking into all my private files, my emails, all my stuff?"

Manya didn't have time for Feliks's tantrums. She'd helped him win the music prize, which was what he wanted, and he should be grateful. The skills she'd discovered through her own investigation were skills she meant to use again. Being able to hack into other computers without being discovered would allow her to find out lots of useful information. The ability to alter that information opened up a whole new world of possibilities. Right now she was in the process of changing her grades. She'd worked out how to get into the main branch of the school system, and it was easy to give herself a grade 'A' from teachers who didn't even know who she was. There was no reason for them to know her as she never attended their lessons. It was surprising that nobody had noticed. Not one teacher had bothered to check why she was missing lessons, no-one had questioned her constant presence in the ICT suite, and nobody had noticed her altered grades. The school system was so easy to hack into, Manya wondered what else she might achieve?

It was disappointing not to have fully mended her friendship with Feliks, but she'd managed on her own before and would manage again. They still sat together for meals, but only discussed safe topics like maths homework or the quality of the food they were eating. Both of their passions were to do with technology, but Feliks didn't want to know about Manya's unauthorised activities, and Manya was baffled by Feliks's absence of ambition and lack of recklessness.

Towards the end of their time at Pushkin, both Manya and Feliks applied to Kolmogorov Boarding School. The special department of the renowned Moscow State University had been established for Moscow's most promising students. The school set its own admission tests, but it was a known fact that students from Pushkin were rarely rejected because they usually achieved such high grades.

Manya wasn't going to achieve high grades unless she knew what the exam questions were going to be. It was one thing tampering with Pushkin's system, but these exams were not going to be internally assessed, they would be sent to Kolmogorov. She needed to see the exam papers and the answers too. She hadn't done any revision, preferring to spend her time working out algorithms to enable her to hack into the complicated systems at the secondary school. So far, she had found them impenetrable.

Then, just two days before the exams, Manya intercepted an email from the Director of Studies at Kolmogorov to her counterpart at Pushkin, explaining how to access the exam papers. There was not enough detail. She needed the password to open the files.

It meant a whole night in her room on her laptop. Even Manya wasn't daring enough to risk breaking into the ICT suite in the dark. By morning, she still hadn't found the code. Without the code, there was no way to access the exam papers. Without the papers, there was no chance of passing the exams. She would leave Pushkin with nothing.

In desperation, Manya went for a walk to clear her head, found herself at the entrance to the school and entered the huge double doors. The flat panel display screens were still showing different parts of the school, and a small twinge of guilt berated her for not having made the most of her time there. She hadn't used the gym, the music rooms or the library, and had never been part of any team.

"Can I help you?" asked the lady behind the reception desk.

Manya saw the computer in front of the woman and made some quick calculations. "Oh, yes please," she answered. "I made a birthday card for my mother, and I need to print it. If I go and get my memory stick, do you think you could print it for me?"

"I don't see why not. You go and get it and if I'm not busy I'll copy it for you."

"Thank you so much," beamed Manya, with what she hoped was a sweet smile.

It took less than three minutes for Manya to upload an AI-generated card onto a new memory stick. 'For Mama, Happy Birthday,' it said. Running back to the entrance hall, she felt the same nervous excitement as when she'd 'helped' Feliks win the music competition. The receptionist was on the phone, but winked at Manya and motioned for her to sit down. It gave Manya time to see that the photocopier was in the room next door. If this was to work, she'd have to be quick, and probably should have thought of something larger than a birthday card. Her heart had started pounding in her chest.

"Now, where is that memory stick, dear," asked the receptionist. "I hope you know how to do this because I don't have a clue how these computers work," she giggled.

Manya went around to the other side of the large counter, looked at the screen and inserted the USB with a trembling hand. Up flashed the hideous, pink birthday card.

"Oh, that is lovely!" squirmed the receptionist. "Your mama will be thrilled to bits when she receives this."

"Thank you," said Manya. "If you wouldn't mind going to the printer, it will come out in a moment."

Manya's hand hovered over the 'Print' key, but as the receptionist bustled out of the room, she had some other buttons to press first.

The first step was to click on the 'File' icon at the bottom of the screen to bring up the documents, but there wasn't time to find the exact file, so copying everything to the USB stick was her only option. Manya took a deep breath as the screen went blank for a moment.

In the middle of the screen the word 'loading' came up, closely followed by 'copying docs...20%...30%'.

"Has it come through yet?" Manya called to the receptionist.

"I can't see it. Shall I come and help you?"

"No!" shouted Manya, abruptly. "I mean, no thanks, it should arrive any second."

'75%.... 99%.... complete,' the screen told Manya, who closed down the window, flicked back to the birthday card and pressed 'Print'.

"Oh, here it comes," called the receptionist. "It looks fabulous!"

Manya almost forgot to wait for the woman to bring the card back out, she was in such a hurry to leave.

She rushed back to her room, inserted the USB, double checked the door was locked, and pushed a chair against it for good measure. The list of files appearing on the screen seemed to go on forever, and Manya couldn't see anything remotely connected with Kolmogorov. It was going to be a long night.

Manya had pushed many boundaries at Pushkin, but stealing exam papers was by far the most daring thing she'd ever done. It made her shudder to think what might happen if anyone found out.

Eleven

England, the present

It was odd to think about following Jude home from school when only a few days ago he'd been following *me*.

The timing was perfect because Big Ben and Tyrone had homework detentions after school which meant Jude would be walking home on his own. I hung back in the classroom for a moment at the end of the day so he wouldn't think I was stalking him.

I watched him turn left out of school, hoping he'd go through the park where it would be easier to follow him, but he continued along the pavement as far as the corner shop and went in. Obviously, I couldn't go in too, so now I had a problem as I didn't know where to wait without looking suspicious. I was about to squeeze into a gap between a wall and a parked car when I heard a voice.

"Billy, whatcha doing here?"

It was Elliot. He's in my class and was standing in front of me offering a Haribo. This was good, I wouldn't look out of place talking to Elliot, so I took a sweet.

"I've switched to Fruitilicious as part of my new fitness regime," he said.

I tried to position myself so that I could see the door of the corner shop, but keep Elliot in front as cover. Elliot was talking about macronutrients and the cardiovascular system and I tried to look interested, while working out where to stand so Jude wouldn't see me when he came out of the shop. Every time the door opened I ducked behind Elliot.

"You alright?" said Elliot. "Are you hiding from someone?" He turned round to see what I was looking at and at that moment Jude came out drinking a can of coke.

"Nah, it's all good but I gotta go," I said as casually as I could. "See ya."

Luckily Jude hadn't seen me and was walking back towards the park, so I shoved my hands in my pockets and followed him, trying to look laid-back. Elliot was still watching me, but it didn't matter. What mattered was to focus on locating Jude's dad; the first step to finding my parents.

As I turned into the park, I thought I'd lost him, but he was standing by the edge of the lake, kicking a stone and draining the remains of his coke. From behind a hedge, I watched him look across the water, aim his can at a duck and launch it like a missile. The can made a splash, and the duck scuttered off across the water unharmed.

I noticed a couple of people settling themselves on park benches, carefully spreading out sheets of newspaper and lying on top of them. I'd heard about homeless people, but I didn't know there were any right here in this park. They were actually going to be sleeping on the benches. It made me feel bad, but I didn't know what I could do to help. One man was singing and playing a small guitar with a cup in front of him for people to put money in. I was surprised to see Jude walk towards him. Was he going to put some money in the cup?

The man with the guitar gave Jude a nod, but Jude ignored him, walked up to the cup and kicked it, sending coins flying everywhere. The guitar man stood up, yelling at Jude and hurriedly collecting up his scattered money. I would have helped, but Jude was turning into an alleyway and I couldn't lose him now. I followed.

The alleyway came out onto a newish estate with semi-detached and terraced houses. After a few minutes, Jude stopped by a low wall, pulled a key out of his pocket and stepped towards the front door of a house with no lights. He turned the key, kicked open the door and flicked a switch all in one movement. I jumped back, thinking the light would show me up, but Jude had already shut the door and another light came on upstairs. A bare bulb was hanging down from the ceiling and the window was cracked, held together with brown tape.

Crossing the road, I sat on a wall behind a post box for a while to see if anything would happen. After about ten minutes I gave up and started back, thinking how different it was for me and Jude when we got home from school. He had to let himself into a dark, quiet, empty house, whereas my home was always full of light, noise, activity and people excited to see me, wanting to hear about my day.

I didn't reckon Jude had a tray of cakes waiting for him.

The image of Jude going into his empty house in the dark stayed with me and I wondered if it was the same for him every night, but feeling sorry for him wasn't an option at this point. It certainly wasn't going to get in the way of the search for his dad who must surely be the key to finding my parents.

Another school trip had been arranged. This time it was the Safety Centre, and I thought it might be a chance to tell Katie about the fire, my missing parents and Jude's kidnapping dad. We managed to sit a few rows behind Jude's gang so we could keep an eye on them, but I knew immediately the coach wouldn't be the right place to discuss anything confidential.

Jude and Tyrone were tearing their Safety Centre leaflets into little pieces and throwing them over Saira and Mina's heads. Big Ben was tearing crusts off a loaf of bread and throwing them into his mouth while Elliot tried to explain the evils of too many carbs.

When we arrived at the centre, Katie and I were the last to jump down from the coach, and as we crossed the car park I was surprised to see a fire-engine. Was Louis here? I wished I'd told him I was coming, it would be great to introduce him to Katie and some of the others.

Mrs Beaman put us into groups and told us we were very lucky because the fire-brigade had come to help out, and the house fire presentation would be led by a real firefighter.

Jude was in my group, but Katie wasn't. We were taken inside and shown how to throw a life ring if we saw someone in a lake, how to check our house for dangerous electrical equipment, and then someone in the group was invited to make a 999 call. Jude was chosen. He was told to go into a phone box, pick up the receiver and press 999 on the keypad. He was supposed to say, "My name is Jude, I am at the corner of Palmar Avenue and Bassett Close and there is a fire at number seventy-two." A man in another room at the safety centre would pretend to be the emergency services and ask questions, but when Jude went into the phone box, he had a strange smirk on his face as he dialled the number. He said, "Hi, my house is on fire. But don't rush 'cos it's only Grandma left inside, and she doesn't matter 'cos she's well old."

I suddenly felt very hot, as though I was standing on my head and all the blood had rushed into it. Inside my head I could see flames everywhere, and I could hear people shouting.

"My boy, my little boy's up there," I heard a woman's voice screaming.

And then, "Quick in here, there's a kid!" shouted a man's voice, and I felt as though I was being carried. Suddenly, a massive noise exploded in my ears, my legs collapsed under me, and I don't remember what happened next...

Twelve

Russia, two years ago

Manya was finishing packing when her father put his head round the door. "Are you nearly ready to leave?" he asked.

"Papa, I'm nearly fifteen, I can manage a train journey by myself. It's too far for you to drive there and back in a day."

"I've got a business meeting in Moscow. I'm going anyway," he said.

Manya didn't want her father to take her to school, but she couldn't think of an excuse.

"I'd like to see the school anyway," he continued. "You know you're the first Molchalin to get into Kolmogorov. You are going to make the name Molchalin great."

"Yes, I know, you keep telling me," said Manya. "And I bet you've been telling anyone who will listen," she added.

Mr Molchalin didn't even notice the sarcasm. He couldn't wait to spread the news that his daughter had secured a place at one of Russia's most prestigious academic establishments.

Manya felt slightly guilty that Papa was so proud. Her exam results had been fabulous, but only because she'd downloaded all the answers first. She was pleased with herself for having cracked the system, but a persistent voice in the back of her head kept scolding, "Manya, you are a cheat."

And she knew whose voice it was. Feliks's. He had secured a place too, but he had gained his through sheer hard work. Despite the thought of Feliks's judgement, she was looking forward to seeing him almost as much as she was looking forward to getting away from her parents. Her mother had ignored her as usual, right through the holidays and her father had been too tied up with his business, whatever that was, he never spoke about it.

She had spent the past two months working on her IT skills, knowing how demanding the courses at her new school were likely to be. Even though her entry into the school had been gained through unconventional means, she was determined to learn as much as she could at Kolmogorov.

Feliks had no idea how Manya had passed all her exams, but he was generous enough to message, *Well done c u there.*

If Mr Molchalin hadn't had time for his daughter throughout the long summer holiday, he appeared to be trying to make up for it now.

"Tell me all about the syllabus," he said as soon as he got in the car. And then, "Do you know anyone else going to Kolmogorov? Any good contacts?"

Manya rolled her eyes at the question, although her father couldn't see. *Why is it always about the contacts?*

"Don't get involved with the wrong crowd."

As his questions and advice droned on, Manya zoned out. *Why is he suddenly so interested in my well-being anyway?*

Mr Molchalin wanted to take a detour past Moscow's prestigious university. "Did you know that ninety-nine percent of Kolmogorov students continue their studies at Moscow State University?" he said.

Manya did know and was pretty sure she'd be the one percent who didn't continue. *I want to get on with my life,* she thought. *I'm going to learn all the skills I need at school.*

But as they approached the university, she couldn't help staring at the enormous white building with its towers and spires.

"Whose is the statue?" she asked, dazzled by the magnificence in front of her.

"That is Mikhail Lomonosov, the founder of Moscow State," said her father. "A brilliant scientist and writer."

The building was at least twenty stories high, leaving the tall pine trees in the gardens completely dwarfed by the construction. When they reached Kolmogorov, the school, despite its imposing main building, felt rather small and inadequate in comparison.

An older student greeted them at the reception desk and led them across a grassy quad to Manya's new bedroom. Mr Molchalin helped carry the bags and they stood awkwardly together in her room. "What time is your meeting, Papa?" she asked.

"Early afternoon. I'm afraid I won't be able to stay to help you find your way around."

"No problem, I'll be fine," Manya replied, rather too quickly.

At Pushkin, Manya's room had been close to Feliks's, and she had felt comforted to know he was nearby. At Kolmogorov, the girls' boarding house was totally separate from the boys', and the subjects Feliks had chosen to study were so different from Manya's that they were not in any of the same classes. But Manya's main concern was to find where the best computers were kept and where the quickest internet was to be found. Friends had never been important to her and she didn't bother to attend the social events put on by the school during the first few days of term.

One morning, Feliks sent a message asking Manya to sit with him for lunch. She was surprised at how much she was looking forward to seeing him and was determined to be friendly.

"So how's the music tech course going?" she asked.

"Fantastic," he replied. "We're looking at music in great Hollywood films."

Manya couldn't think of anything more boring.

"Wow! That must be interesting," she said, trying to sound sincere.

"It is. One day I'm going to win an Oscar for writing the musical score for a great Russian film," he said. "How's computer science? I hope you're not up to your old tricks again, hacking into people's private business."

"Of course not," lied Manya. "I'm making a lovely little game for small children called 'Grow up to be a Geek.'"

"Manya, I'm being serious. I'm the only person who knows what you can do, and you'd better keep it that way or you're going to get into a lot of trouble."

Manya found the work on her course disappointingly easy. She had already worked out complicated coding, knew how to create algorithms, and certainly didn't feel the need to attend an 'Introduction to AI'.

Once again she found herself skipping lessons, but didn't intend to sit around doing nothing. Most of her time was spent trying to gain access to illegal networks, reading private messages between other students and, if she was really bored, creating amusing AI graphics.

One investigation took her to the university schedule where one particular module caught her eye: 'Cyber Security'. Now that could be useful if she could firstly get there, secondly, attend the university lectures without being missed at school and thirdly, pass as a university student.

She needn't have worried; a regular bus from just outside school took fifteen minutes to get to Kolmogorov. Manya discovered it one afternoon while missing a Programming Languages lesson. Having arrived at the campus, she studied the clothes worn by the older students and found a mixed bunch, some of them looking even younger than Manya herself. A pair of jeans and a baseball cap would be a good enough disguise.

As she wandered around the campus, her courage grew and she slipped into a lecture theatre behind a group of girls. She sat with her head lowered at the end of a row of students, but she'd picked a pure maths lecture, and had to sit for an hour and a half listening to the properties and structure of abstract objects, which meant nothing to her at all.

Two weeks after her arrival at Kolmogorov, Manya attended her first Computer Security lecture. This was more like it!

Having completed 'Cyber Attacks', a new module began which she found even more compelling, "War-time Technology". Manya was thrilled to discover how Russian cipher officers were considered the heroes and heroines of the Second World War. She would never forget the day when Professor Yenin, head of computer science, stood at the front of the huge lecture theatre and told the students about how, during World War II, the Germans were unable to decipher even one Soviet encrypted message.

"It was one of the most remarkable technological achievements in history, and contributed to the eventual defeat of Germany," explained Professor Yenin.

How Manya would have loved being part of that team! Devising impenetrable secret messages during the war must have been the best job in the world.

"I've got a dream too," Manya told Feliks next time she met up with him. "One day, a lecturer will tell his students that Manya Molchalin was responsible for the most remarkable technological achievement in history."

"And what will that be?" Feliks asked.

"I haven't worked that bit out yet," she replied.

Now that Manya had a new goal, she spent many hours reading about encryption, code breaking and spies, and decided to try a little spying of her own. She started with Feliks and learned that he would be going on a music tour of Austria with some of the students on his music course. She wasn't pleased to see he was communicating regularly with a girl called Karine and was irritated to find that she cared. She turned her attention to something more appealing, and one evening found herself logging into a University student chat named 'Goar V'. A quick search showed Manya that Goar Vartanyan was a Russian spy who uncovered a German plot to kill Winston Churchill and Franklin Roosevelt during World War II. What excited Manya was that Goar was a woman.

Manya was able to intercept messages between the Goar V group which seemed to have activated a little spy ring of their own. Something to do with space technology. It wasn't exactly clear what they were up to, but logging in at midnight every night became a habit. Within a few weeks she had uncovered the name of the leader of Goar V, and soon after that, she found her photo. It became a game for Manya to see if she could spot Tatiana during her illicit visits to the university lecture theatres. She even spent time at the various gyms around the campus; not to do any exercise, just to keep a look out for the young woman with short, bleached hair. Tatiana always wore black and spent much of her free time working with huge weights in the gym and running for endless miles on the treadmill.

One evening, just after midnight, Manya was in her room trying to connect to Goar V when there was a knock on the door. She couldn't remember when anyone had knocked on her door before and wondered who it could be. For a split second she hoped it might be Feliks, but then she remembered he was on his music tour with Karine.

"Who is it?" she called through the door.

No answer.

"Is somebody there?" she asked again, feeling anxious.

No answer.

Suddenly a confident voice penetrated the silence.

"Open the door, Manya."

Terrified, Manya opened the door to see a familiar face standing in front of her...

Thirteen

England, the present

I awoke to find myself lying on the floor, on top of a big pile of coats. Mrs Beaman was sitting on a chair a bit too close to me, looking worried.

"Billy," she said, "are you alright? The man leading your group said you fainted."

For a moment I couldn't think where I was. Then I saw Katie standing near Mrs Beaman and she was looking worried too.

"What happened?" she asked. "Saira told me your face went all red and your legs collapsed."

The Safety Centre! That's where I was. Jude had been making that phone call and he'd said something about letting his Gran go up in flames because she was old.

What had happened in my head? It was like a dream, but it wasn't a dream, it was more of a memory. Was I remembering the fire at my house from when I was two? Was it my mum's voice?

"I'm okay," I said, not feeling okay. "Where's everyone else?"

The others were eating lunch together. Katie and I had ours with the teachers which wasn't much fun. In fact, it was really awkward and nobody spoke, but soon it was time to get back in our groups for the last activity. Jude was in trouble again and had to stay in the lunch hall with one of the volunteers, while the rest of us were led to the house which was supposed to be on fire.

"And I'm proud to introduce you all to a real firefighter," said the volunteer. Everyone looked impressed as the firefighter came to the front. He looked pretty cool in his uniform, but it wasn't Louis.

The firefighter probably gave a good talk about what to do if there was a fire in your house and how to make sure you had a smoke alarm, but I wasn't really listening. I knew about house fires, and I knew what firefighters did when they were on duty. I was thinking that if I could remember the fire now, then maybe I would begin to remember other things, like the names of my parents, and what they looked like.

At the end of our visit, we lined up and thanked the volunteers. Jude was looking angry again and he tried to slip into the queue in front of Big Ben who gave him a kick in the back of the legs. Mrs Beaman opened the door, counting us out, and as we made our way across the car park, Big Ben gave Jude a push from behind. Jude turned round to punch him. They both staggered sideways and stumbled towards the moving wheels of a second fire engine which was pulling into the car park.

Mrs Beaman screamed.

The fire engine stopped dead, the door of the cab opened, the driver jumped out and ran round to where Jude and Big Ben were standing looking stupid.

It was Louis.

"What do you think you're doing, fooling around in a car park?" he said to Jude and Big Ben, angrily. "You've just come out of the Safety Centre! Didn't you listen to anything they told you in there?"

Jude and Big Ben's faces had changed from white to the colour of ketchup. Mrs Beaman started to apologise, "I'm so sorry..." but Louis was already striding towards the building. At that point he saw me and his face broke into a smile.

"Billy mate, I didn't know you were here today, why didn't you tell me?"

"Hey Louis," I said, trying to sound cool as he came over for a fist bump.

"I'm coming round later. See ya." He turned around again and walked away.

Everyone had gone quiet, they were all looking at me. Most of them had their mouths open and their eyes wide. Even Mrs Beaman.

"D...do you know him, Billy?" she stuttered, still flustered at the idea of having two of her pupils squashed by a fire engine.

"Yeah, that's my mate, Louis," I replied.

There was a hushed sort of awe as we got back into the coach. Jude had to sit next to Mrs Beaman and Big Ben had to sit next to Miss Newton which would ruin his plans to eat any food he still had in his bag.

Katie sat down next to me. "Do you know that firefighter? How do you know him? Why is he coming to visit you?"

"He's Louis, my friend, and I'll tell you about him later...when nobody is listening!" I added in a loud voice for the benefit of Tyrone whose ear I could see pressed between the two seats in front.

Katie and I sat in silence. This would surely be the chance to tell her about my parents. I had the whole journey to think about how to say it and what order to put it in without sounding too over-dramatic, but by the time we got back to school I still hadn't made up my mind what to say.

Katie grabbed my arm almost as soon as we were out of the coach. "Go on then, you said you'd tell me about the firefighter. Why don't I come to your house sometime, and you can introduce me?"

I took a deep breath. "Look Katie, I don't actually live in a house."

"Okay, your apartment, your bungalow, the place where you live."

"I live in an old people's home." There, I'd said it.

There was silence while Katie digested my news.

After a very long pause Katie said, "That is so cool!"

Cool. She thought it was cool!

"Wow Billy, why didn't you tell me before? What's it like?"

I told Katie about the fire, my parents, Autumn Days, the Oldies and about Gran.

"Can I come? I really want to meet all these people and see your room and everything."

Katie didn't mind that I lived in an old people's home. She hadn't laughed at me. She thought it was cool! We made a plan for her to come round on Saturday to help with my investigations.

Fourteen

Russia, one-and-a-half years ago

Manya looked at the figure standing in front of her.

Tatiana.

Having followed Tatiana for so long and listened to so many of the group conversations, even though she'd never actually spoken to the formidable young woman, Manya felt she knew her. Close-up, Tatiana was smaller than Manya expected, but with a steely, almost devouring expression she hadn't observed from a distance.

"Hello, Manya," said Tatiana.

How does she know my name? thought Manya, her heart beating, her mouth dry.

"Hello. C...C...Come in," she managed.

Tatiana waited until Manya had shut the door behind them before speaking again.

"Quite the little spy, aren't we?" she said, patronisingly.

"Look, I'm really sorry," said Manya. "I just stumbled on your group, and I thought all the things you were talking about sounded really interesting."

"Don't even begin to think you can lie to me, Manya Molchalin. Ever," said Tatiana in a firm and steady voice. "I know you found us through a deliberate search. I know how long you've been tuning into our meetings, I know when you started following us and I know every time you watch me training."

Manya couldn't speak. *How did she know?* She had been so careful to keep a distance.

"In fact, Manya, you will not have realised this, but we invited you to find us. I noticed your covert activities some weeks ago and I was impressed by your ability to access so many of the University files and documents which are supposed to be secure. That *are* secure to everyone except the more advanced Black Hats."

"What's a Black Hat?" ventured Manya.

"A Black Hat is someone who breaks into computer networks with malicious intent. And that's what you've been doing. In fact, you're showing great potential." Tatiana smiled for the first time. Manya wasn't sure if the smile was friendly, so she didn't smile back.

"I'll stop following you, I promise," she faltered.

"No!" snapped Tatiana. "Don't you understand? The reason I'm standing here right now is because you've been chosen."

"Chosen?"

"You've shown great skill in your ability to break into the secrets of computers. Your interest in Soviet encryption during the war shows your passion for learning. I am here to invite you to join Goar V."

Manya blinked. "What do I have to do?" she asked.

"First, let me see your phone," said Tatiana, holding out her hand. Manya hesitated, but the look on Tatiana's face told her that refusal was not an option. She reached into her pocket and passed it over.

"I like the way you've done your room," said Tatiana, her tone suddenly more friendly. "It must be a good view from that window when it's light."

Manya glanced over her shoulder. *The view? Why is she talking about the view?* She turned round again to see Tatiana examining her phone.

"Just as I thought, we'll have to upgrade you."

Manya felt a sudden wave of apprehension. "What if I don't want to join?" she said. "What if I'm quite happy on my own?"

"Believe me, Manya, you need us," said Tatiana. "I know about your mother and her secret obsessions. I know how you achieved straight 'A' grades to gain your place here. I've been observing you for a long time, you'd be foolish to refuse. Not only because we're not accustomed to being refused, but also because, by joining Goar V you will be opening yourself to opportunities you couldn't even begin to imagine."

"What do you mean?"

"You've already worked out that we are involved in a highly confidential Space Tech programme. Let me put it this way:

we can use a student with your skills, and in return you will have access to information seen by very few people in Russia. At Pushkin you were encouraged to love the Motherland. It was always assumed that you would give something back to the Motherland."

Tatiana walked towards the door.

"But wait!" pleaded Manya. "I don't know what you want me to do!"

"Nothing. You need to think about this carefully. I trust you won't need me to tell you how to contact me. But you might need this." She threw Manya's phone onto her bed. "I have a good feeling about you, Manya, I don't think you're going to let me down."

Tatiana slipped out of the door and closed it silently behind her.

Manya stood for a moment trying to replay the scene. Had Tatiana, from the Goar V group, just offered her a place in the team? What was expected of her? What should she do?

She lay on her bed going over and over Tatiana's words. At some point she must have fallen asleep because when she opened her eyes, dawn was breaking.

Should I tell Feliks? she wondered, sadly realising that he was the only person in the world who might listen to her and give her advice. Up until last night, she had been totally focused on her own path, satisfied that she was making progress in her own time and in her own way. Yes, she had mastered a useful skill in accessing secret information, but it had always been on her terms and under her control. Tatiana made her nervous. If she joined Goar V she would be in a team, and she'd never been any good at group work at school. She simply didn't like other people. They always judged her and questioned her decisions. On the other hand, if she refused, Tatiana had implied something bad would happen. She resolved to find Feliks as soon as he got back from his music tour.

"What did you think I was going to say, Manya?" Feliks exclaimed a few days later. "You tell me that some weirdo from some freakish gang is threatening you and you're not sure what is the right thing to do! Honestly Manya, I know you've always had an issue with knowing what's right and wrong, but this is a whole new level. You need to cut all contact with this Tatiana and get back to studying what you're here for. Forget about them, they're dangerous."

"But I haven't told you what the group is doing. She offered to..."

There was a quiet knock on the door, and it opened straight away. Feliks jumped up and walked towards Karine.

"Oh, sorry," said Karine, blushing, "I didn't know you were busy."

"It's fine," said Feliks, looking pointedly at Manya. "Manya was just leaving. You know what I think. Just forget about the whole thing, Manya." He put his hand on the open door as if encouraging her departure.

Manya slunk back across the quad to her room. She was angry that Feliks had dismissed her so abruptly in favour of Karine. He didn't know anything. As she went to her desk and opened her laptop a message appeared.

Don't ever discuss our work with anyone again.

Manya had no choice. She was scared of Tatiana, and she had become too involved to back out now. What would the Goar V team do to her if she refused?

On reflection, she was rather proud to have been selected. They recognized her potential, and she didn't want to let them down. After all, this was what she'd been working up to her whole life. She allowed herself to dream about the possibilities of being part of a Russian spy ring. Something to do with space technology, Tatiana had said. Maybe one day the Motherland would uphold her, Manya Molchalin, as a key figure in helping Russia to lead the Space Race.

Having made up her mind, Manya went to see if Tatiana was at the gym, but there was no sign of her, so she sat in a corner to wait. After three long hours she decided to go for a walk to stretch her legs. When she returned to her corner, she found a small envelope on the chair with the letters MM on the front. Manya Molchalin? Manya whipped her head round to see a small figure in black leggings disappearing through the door.

How did she know I was here? Manya wondered as she pocketed the paper and made her way back to school. On the bus she opened the paper, her fingers trembling.

There was a phone number and the words, "It's raining in Moscow, and I forgot my umbrella."

That was all. What could this mean?

She rushed back to her room and dialled the number.

"Yes?" said a voice.

"It's raining in Moscow, and I forgot my umbrella," breathed Manya.

"Keep your phone with you at all times," said the voice, and the call was disconnected.

For a whole week, Manya had trouble concentrating, and every time she felt her phone vibrate it made her jump.

One afternoon, walking alone back to her room, a small figure appeared next to her, seemingly out of nowhere.

"Keep walking and listen," whispered Tatiana. "We have decided to give you an opportunity to serve the Motherland, but you will need to make a few sacrifices. Firstly, you must not tell anyone where you are going or what you are doing, and that includes family."

No problem at all, Manya thought to herself, but remained silent.

"You'll stay here until we're ready for you, and then you'll be called for training."

"What sort of training? Will I have to miss school?" asked Manya.

"Don't ask stupid questions. If you're committed, you'll be ready at all times." Tatiana made as if to leave but Manya grabbed her arm.

"Just tell me how you seem to know where I am all the time," she said.

Tatiana looked at her disdainfully. "I am surprised at you, Manya," she said. "For someone so devious, you're not showing much intelligence." Think back to the day I came to your room and asked to see your phone. Do you remember when I commented on the view? You turned away and it gave me time to insert a tracker and a microphone. We've been monitoring you ever since. Use this as a lesson to never turn your back. Don't trust anyone. You're going to destroy your current phone and take this one. Remember, I promised you an upgrade?"

"I suppose this has an inbuilt tracker and microphone too?" asked Manya.

Tatiana gave Manya another look of disdain and slipped away.

I'll take that as a yes then.

To begin with, Manya felt special. Tatiana had selected her, and she was accepted as part of a team that promised to achieve great things. She wasn't sure yet what was expected of her, but she would make sure to be ready for whatever they asked her to do.

After a few weeks, Manya began to feel jittery. She knew the phone Tatiana had given her was keeping track of everywhere she went, everything she said, and everything she did. It made her feel self-conscious about speaking to, or messaging anyone for fear of being judged and analysed by Goar V. Sometimes she left her phone in her room just to get away from it, but didn't dare stay away for too long in case they found out.

Manya had never been a sociable person and it hadn't really bothered her before, but she missed Feliks. Should she have taken his advice and backed off while she still had the chance?

Little by little Manya's anxiety grew. She spent long hours alone in her room, only venturing out for the few lessons she was still enrolled in, and occasionally to the library after most of the other students had left. Even the university lectures she had enjoyed so much were dropped in case Tatiana called her for her mission. It was important to be ready at all times.

Manya stopped taking lunch in the school dining room with the other students. Firstly because it was busy with people she didn't know, secondly, there was a chance of bumping into someone she *did* know. It meant occasionally taking the short walk to the school tuck shop to stock up with food, but she always wore her baseball cap with the large visor which could be pulled down over her face. On one of these trips, Manya was aware of a group of students approaching and kept her head firmly down.

"Manya?"

It was Feliks. Manya raised her head a little. What if Tatiana was listening? She wanted to talk to Feliks, but not while she had her phone in her pocket.

"Manya?" he repeated. "Are you okay?"

She nodded, but said nothing. Suddenly she felt annoyed with herself. *Why shouldn't I talk to Feliks?* She reached into her pocket and turned off her phone.

"It's good to see you Feliks," she said, relaxing. "How is the great composer? Have you written your masterpiece yet?"

It felt so easy to talk to Feliks. Normal. He told her about his work and asked how her studying was going.

"All good," she lied.

"So you've given up the spying idea then?" he said.

Manya suddenly felt very hot; she needed to get away.

"Manya," continued Feliks, "please tell me you're not still involved with those..."

"Sorry Feliks," interrupted Manya, "I need to be...erm... somewhere."

Sprinting away from Feliks, Manya fled to her room and turned on her phone. Immediately a message flashed up on her screen.

Do NOT turn off your phone when you are out. We know exactly where you are and who you are talking to. Be very careful.

Manya threw the phone onto the bed. She stood by the window and looked out, wondering how she could have let herself get into this situation. She looked at students walking past, laughing and chatting with their friends. They were so happy and free. She wanted to be free too.

She began to think about her mother and how she had cut herself off from the world long ago. How had it started for her? Her mother was irrational, there was no doubt about it, but was she, Manya, heading the same way?

Over the next few weeks Manya felt herself sinking down into a deeper and deeper depression and there was nothing she could do to stop it. Then, one night, she had a dream.

She was back at home with Babushka. Babushka was teaching her how to bake a Russian honey cake and Manya was stirring the mixture. As she watched the gooey mess revolving around the bowl, a Mendelssohn concerto began to play and a tiny figure appeared at the edge. The figure continued to rotate, growing bigger with every second. It was Mrs Molchalin. Manya dropped the spoon and stepped back, but the mixture kept spinning on its own.

Suddenly, her mother reached a hand towards Manya as if asking to be pulled out. Manya grasped her mother's arm, but instead of trying to get out, Mrs Molchalin was pulling her back towards the bowl. Manya felt herself being dragged into the spiralling mixture...

She awoke with a jolt. *I am not heading the same way as her, I'm not!*

Quickly pulling on a pair of leggings, Manya ran through the darkness of the night all the way to the lake at the far end of the school grounds.

She paused, looking into the mysterious, still water and the reflection of the moon amongst the bulrushes enticing her forwards.

Come on, she urged herself, *I have to do this!*

Fifteen

England, the present

I arrived home from the school trip to a screeching sound which could be heard from the bottom of the stairs.

"I tell you, somebody stole it," Beryl was yelling. "It was on my dressing table and now it's gone!"

Neelam needed help, so I ran over to take Beryl's other arm and lead her to a chair.

"What's going on?" I asked.

"My bracelet!" Beryl yelled into my ear. "There's a dirty thief in the house!"

Neelam looked at Beryl with her patient face. "Don't worry Beryl, we'll find it." Then she turned to me, shaking her head wearily. "She's accused just about everybody."

Gran was sitting in her wheelchair with a pink face and looking unhappy. It was a good moment to get away from the mayhem, and I pushed her to the lift, grabbing a couple of rugs on the way.

I took Gran to the ground floor and out into the garden where the sun was shining. She perked up immediately and started pointing at the spring flowers and the pigeons which were pecking at the grass. Something caught my eye, it was my green football, the one I thought I'd lost, so I left Gran for a few seconds to retrieve it.

Turning back, I could see Gran examining something shiny, something gold, and as I got closer my heart nearly jumped out of my mouth. It was a bracelet. Gran was running it round her wrinkled old fingers and humming a little tune.

"Gran, where did you find that bracelet?"

She looked at me, trying to process what I'd just said.

"Well, I think it was on the train," she said. "Yes, and she had a little dog on her knee."

The expression on her face was as though she'd just got a complicated maths question right and I knew one thing for sure, Gran wasn't going to be able to tell me where she found that bracelet.

I sat with her in the garden, trying to work out how Beryl's bracelet could possibly have got into her hands. Gran would never steal anything.

When we went back up, Beryl was still shouting. This time she was pointing at Mary.

"I know it's you! Give it back!"

Either Mary couldn't hear, or she was ignoring Beryl. She just sat calmly, twiddling her beads and gently nodding her head.

I went to fetch a cup of tea for Gran which was a big mistake because, while I was gone, she held up the bracelet and of course, Beryl's beady eyes spotted it straightaway.

She hobbled over to Gran, wagging her finger. "You thief! I should call the police."

Gran looked up at Beryl, beaming. "I used to have such lovely nails," she said. "Now look at them." She held out her hands to show Beryl, who stopped shouting for a moment and looked at her own hands.

"But what in the world is this thingumyjoodle?" asked Gran, noticing the bracelet wrapped around her fingers as though she'd never seen it before. Beryl used the opportunity to keep shouting, and I looked over to Frank who was sitting in his chair with his arms folded across his chest, clearly enjoying every minute of the drama.

Then something very unexpected happened. Mandy appeared from the kitchen, marched directly over to Beryl, grabbed both her arms and levered her into the nearest armchair.

“Enough!” she said, and walked back to the kitchen.

Beryl was so surprised, she stopped ranting and leaned back on the cushions, grumbling to herself.

Frank leaned towards me. “Blinking Rusky,” he muttered, “I bet she was the one who stole the bracelet.”

Beryl soon had her bracelet safely back on her wrist, and everything calmed down. Mandy brought out the tea with her special Sachertorte cake, and I suddenly felt ravenous, not having eaten much lunch at the Safety Centre. I took three plates of cake over to Gran and Frank, ready to tell them about my trip, but just as I was about to speak, the door to Nostalgia opened and in walked Louis.

Everything went silent.

“Hi guys,” he said in his usual greeting.

All the old ladies love Louis. When he arrives, they sit up straighter and pat their hair. Louis did the rounds, chatting to all of them briefly, before coming to sit with us holding a big slice of cake.

"What's all this about Beryl's bracelet?" he asked.

I explained what had happened.

"Maybe Beryl dropped it on a bush when she went outside and Gran must have picked it up," he suggested.

"That's what I thought," I replied. "But Neelam said Beryl hasn't been in the garden today, or at all this week."

"It's a mystery," said Louis. "But how was the Safety Centre? Are those two numbskulls friends of yours? I hope I didn't embarrass you."

"Jude a friend of mine? No chance! It was hilarious when you told them off."

Louis smiled and finished his cake. "Billy," he said. "I've got to go now, but I'll come back soon, and we'll play football in the park. Look after yourself."

As Louis left, Pascal came floating down the corridor from his bedroom twisting his hands and wailing in his French accent, "My golden tie pin, it has gone! I wasn't wearing a tie dis morning because I was doing my exercises, but jus now I changed and, oh la la, look at my poor tie, all floppy wizout a pin!"

Over the weekend, lots of other things started to go missing on the Nostalgia floor. After Pascal's tie pin it was Mary's beads, then Neelam's silver hairclip and even Frank's gold watch. I secretly looked for all of it in Gran's room and it made me feel guilty. I didn't think she could have stolen anything, but I couldn't forget she was the one who found Beryl's bracelet.

Sixteen

Russia, one year ago

Manya stood by the lake, considering her options. If she carried this through, she risked being abandoned by Tatiana.

"Think about how you will be able to help the Motherland!" Tatiana had said.

"One day you will make the name Molchalin great!" her father had said.

But what about her mother? *I am not going to end up like her!* Digging her hand into her pocket, Manya pulled out her phone, the one Tatiana had given her. It was impossible to live like this, being watched all the time. Waiting and waiting to be summoned for training, whatever that was. It would drive her insane.

It was time to finish this nightmare once and for all.

Gripping the phone, Manya yanked her arm back, a surge of rebellion coursing through her veins. With a cry of defiance, she flung it forward with all her might. The phone arced through the air, a tiny silhouette against the dark sky. It hung, suspended for a heart-stopping moment, then plunged into the inky water with a final gurgle. Ripples erupted on the surface, expanding like silent screams, daring her to chase after the source of her torment.

She waited until the last ripple had disappeared and then, with a whoop of joy, she ran back up the hill in the direction of Feliks's room. She felt free.

Manya spent the rest of term trying to enjoy herself with Feliks and his friends, but she couldn't help wondering what the consequences would be for not following Tatiana's rules.

The spring holidays were spent alone at home. Her mother permanently shut in her room, her father out 'on business' most days, and most nights for that matter. Manya preferred it that way; when he was at home, he questioned her relentlessly.

"How is the studying? Your report shows A grades, but there are no comments from the teachers. Have you joined the gym? Have you met Anatoli Ilyich? His mother works at Gazprom. Or Yelizaveta Zakharova? Her grandfather is chairman of Sberbank.

Mrs Molchalin only emerged from her bedroom to refill her coffee cup. Manya spent her days alone, studying in her room and eating meals at the heavy, wooden dining table. Occasionally, she would watch a film in the Molchalin's small living room with the volume turned up to drown out the sound of her mother's music. Once or twice, mother and daughter found themselves in the kitchen together, but neither spoke. Each behaved as though the other didn't exist.

After a week of doing nothing, Manya grew bored. Despite her efforts, she couldn't stop her mind wandering to Tatiana and Goar V and began to search online for information about the group, its members and its mission. However, it was as though Goar V had never existed and that in itself was beguiling enough to cast doubts in Manya's mind. Had she made the wrong decision about Tatiana? Maybe throwing her phone into the lake had been a big mistake.

One morning, while digging deeper into her investigations, a message came through:

"It's raining by the lake in Lopatinsky Park at 16.00 today and I forgot my umbrella."

Manya felt a thrill of excitement.

The park was within walking distance of the Molchalin's home, and Manya could hardly wait for four o'clock to arrive. She kept going over and over in her head the reason for the meeting.

Is it possible Tatiana could still want me to work for her?

The more she thought about it, the more she wanted it to be true. To spy for her country would be interesting, exciting, maybe even dangerous.

At three-thirty, Manya set off for the park, remembering the last time she'd stood next to a lake, and a cold apprehension entered her mind. *What if Tatiana is angry with me for destroying the phone and losing contact? What if she's come to punish me?* Manya halted and was about to go home, when she spotted a small figure dressed in black, waiting on a bench overlooking the lake. Nervously, Manya approached the bench and sat next to Tatiana.

"Your training begins in three days," said Tatiana, handing over a package.

"What training? I threw your phone in the lake!" exclaimed Manya in astonishment.

"You showed courage and individuality. You might have lost contact with us, but we never lost sight of you, Manya."

"What do you want me to do? I need to know more about Goar V."

"Helping our glorious country should be enough," said Tatiana. "It's every Russian's dream to make the Motherland into a great empire. Goar V is a small, but very important cog in the wheel of a large corporation."

"But what does the corporation do?" asked Manya.

"This is top-secret intelligence," said Tatiana. "Sharing information outside our group is not an option. In fact it is a capital offence."

Manya was shocked. "Do you mean I would be killed if I told anyone?"

Tatiana narrowed her eyes and nodded gravely. "Are you sure you want to know?"

"I need to know," said Manya, realising there would be no going back once she knew the secret.

"In that case we will start walking. We can't risk being overheard."

Tatiana walked close to the edge of the lake and Manya, her heart pounding, fell into step beside her.

"We acquired a British scientist, codename Galileo, who was working on a project to create a telescope powerful enough to see into a black hole. Historically the space race has been a competition between Russia and America to achieve superior space flight and galactic knowledge. To be the first country able to discover the mysteries of a black hole would put Russia ahead of the rest of the world."

Manya felt her eyes widening and her heart beating even faster. But how could she, just a schoolgirl, possibly become involved in such an enormous program.

"Our job is to ensure that Galileo continues to work for us. The scientist is invaluable and irreplaceable. Your task will be to assist our assignment.

"Take this, read it, and buy yourself some decent trainers. I know you can do this."

And with that, she was gone.

Ten days later, Manya was back at school, sitting in her room looking at a message on her phone.

Olga Korbut gym 7pm today

Manya had ripped open the package left by Tatiana straightaway, sitting on the bench in Lopatinsky park. Inside she'd been dismayed to find a pair of black leggings. Having avoided all sporting activity for as long as she could remember, this was not a good start. Tucked inside the clothing was an envelope containing two small rectangular cards. The first was a university gym membership with the name *Manya Surkova* and a headshot. The second was a driving licence with the same name and photo.

Manya was already apprehensive about beginning training, and as she walked towards the gym she could see, through the large windows, students on running machines, weight machines and contraptions that looked more like methods of torture. She almost turned back.

"I am Izolda, your instructor," said a young, muscular woman appearing out of nowhere and looking Manya up and down disdainfully. "I don't need to know your name or anything about you. I've been given three months to whip you into shape, so let's get going."

Izolda looked like the sort of person who would readily use a whip if necessary, and Manya wished she could simply shrivel up and disappear.

For twenty minutes, Manya was taken through an exhausting set of exercises and she was glad when she was told to take a drink.

Well, the first session wasn't too bad, she thought.

"Okay, that's the warm-up," said Izolda. "Now choose a set of dumbbells and show me twenty Romanian deadlifts."

"What's a deadlift," asked Manya, dreading an exercise which included the word 'dead'.

The next morning, Manya was woken at 5.00 by an alarm she hadn't set. She tried to get out of bed to turn it off, but every muscle ached. The session with Izolda had put her body through an endurance test she could never have imagined, and she groaned with pain as she reached out for her mobile.

Front gates 5.30am

Manya didn't think she'd reach the front gates in half an hour. Usually it was a five-minute walk, but today it would feel like a marathon with a couple of flights of stairs thrown in to test her painful legs. What did they expect of her this morning? Not more exercise, surely.

Pulling leggings and a sweatshirt over her pyjamas, Manya staggered down the stairs and out into the cold, gloomy morning. A grey Lada was waiting at the front gates from which a young woman emerged. She came to stand directly in front of Manya, dark glasses covering her eyes, and silver hair falling across one side of her face. The other side of her head was shaved, giving her an air of icy aggression.

"I'm Jana. Get in and don't talk." she ordered.

Manya hesitated. She was on edge and would have run back to school if her legs hadn't felt like lead.

"Did Tatiana ask you to..." began Manya.

A sharp slap stopped her from completing the sentence.

"I said don't talk," said Jana. "Get in."

Manya eased into the passenger seat and had hardly pulled the door shut, before the Lada sped off into the darkness. Manya clutched the edges of the seat as the car swerved first one way, then the other along the narrow, winding lane. Trees ahead seemed to be racing towards them and the car jolted as it left the road and continued along a track. Manya couldn't imagine how it was possible to drive through the dim morning light wearing dark glasses and glanced sideways. There was a wide grin on Jana's face and Manya decided to shut her eyes until the ordeal was over. She couldn't give this madwoman the satisfaction of seeing how frightened she was.

As the car raced along, bumping and skidding, Jana only spoke one word.

"Scared?"

Manya didn't reply and kept her eyes shut. She'd been told not to speak, and she didn't want another slap, she just wanted it to be over. When the car finally lurched to a halt, Manya opened her eyes, relieved to see daylight. They had arrived at a wide tarmacked area which looked as though it might have once been an aeroplane runway.

Jana got out and motioned for Manya to swap seats. Three months of intensive, early-morning driving lessons had begun.

Seventeen

England, the present

School wasn't going well. I'd invited Katie to come to Autumn Days on Monday afternoon, but she went home with some sickness bug and was off school for the whole week. Jude saw it as an opportunity.

At morning break on Wednesday, I was walking towards the playing fields, when I felt someone kick me. I spun round expecting to see Jude, but it was Kyle from the year below. As he ran off laughing, I felt another kick. This time it was Arjun.

"Why did you kick me?" I shouted after him.

Then another kick and another. Surely Jude didn't have everyone on his side!

Mina came up to me and it felt like she was touching my back. I was about to lash out at her, but she calmly pulled something off my jacket and handed it to me. It was a sticky note with the words *Kick me* in big black writing. Jude must have stuck it on as we crowded out of the classroom. I managed a small 'thanks' to Mina who nodded and walked away.

The stupid trick made me angry, and all my generous thoughts towards Jude and his difficult home situation flew out of the window. It made me more determined to step up my investigation into his dad. If I could just find out whether Mr Doyle had been putting pressure on my parents to sell their house, I would know I was on the right lines. Only one person could answer that question and I needed to find a way to talk to him.

My bad mood hadn't lifted when I got home, and it didn't help when the first thing anyone said to me was, "Stop stomping like an elephant, you'll never get a girlfriend."

I ignored Beryl and went over to Gran. Frank was asleep in the next chair, Sellotape plastered all over his jacket across his medals. Maybe he was worried about the 'thief' stealing them, but even that annoyed me. If he was so worried about his medals, why didn't he ask Neelam to lock them in the safe?

Gran was bouncing her doll up and down on her knee, saying, "Dardar, Dardar, Dardar," over and over.

"Gran," I said, holding her hands down so she would have to stop the bouncing. "Gran, I need to ask you a really important question."

She pulled her hands away and went back to bouncing. "Dardar, Dardar."

"Gran, do you remember the house where we lived with Mum and Dad?"

"Dar de dar de Dardar."

"Gran!" I said a bit louder. "Could you just listen for a moment, I need to ask you about our house."

Gran looked at me. "Michael, say hello to Dardar."

"I'm not Michael," I muttered through gritted teeth. "If Michael's your son, you could at least *try* to help me find him!" I knew she couldn't help it and that I was being unreasonable, but sometimes it just got so frustrating.

Neelam appeared behind me. "Billy, what's the matter, this isn't like you."

I put my head in my hands. I hadn't wanted Neelam to hear me talking to Gran like that. Everything was going wrong, and now I'd been mean to Gran.

I ran to my room and dived onto the bed. I didn't want to go to school tomorrow, I wanted to stay at home and get on with the more important job of finding my parents.

I didn't want to have to face Jude. I tried not to let him bother me, but I didn't know what he and his gang were going to do next.

Neelam came in and sat on the bed.

"Billy, do you want to talk about anything?"

I shook my head.

"I don't know what's happened, but I want you to know how special you are to us all," she said. "Do you know how much we look forward to seeing you after school? It's like the sun coming out when you come home."

She left the room, and I felt guilty. I had a home full of people who loved me, who cared about me, unlike Jude who had nobody at home, and a bare lightbulb in his room.

I needed to get a grip and get through to the weekend. By then Katie might be well enough to come round and help me find Jude's dad.

I made it to Friday lunch break with nothing too bad happening. That was until I went outside. I was kicking a ball around with Elliot, when Amy from the year below came over.

"Billy, could you give me a hand? My new pen fell down a hole over there and I can't get it out."

Stupidly, I didn't stop to think that it was suspicious, I simply followed Amy to the edge of the playground where I saw the lid of a drainpipe had been removed.

"Down here?" I asked.

She nodded and ran off.

Why didn't I stop at that point? I was doing the girl a favour and she'd run away, only a complete idiot wouldn't have seen the trap.

Stupidly, I reached down the drain, feeling for the lost pen. A sickening snap sounded, followed by a jolt of searing pain that rocketed up my arm. Gasping, I pulled out my hand and wrenched off the metal contraption that was clinging viciously to my fingers. It was a mouse trap. Angrily, I threw it down and looked over to where Amy was standing at the far side of the playground. Jude was standing beside her with a smug look on his face as he handed her a Twix. Everything clicked into place. Jude had rigged the trap and told Amy she could have the chocolate bar if she tricked me into reaching down the drain.

The throbbing in my arm was excruciating, and all I could think about was getting away. Far away.

I ran out of school and didn't stop until I reached the granite entrance sign to Autumn Days where an ambulance was parked. I stopped briefly, wondering if the paramedics had anything to stop the pain in my fingers, but nobody was around so I went inside and up the stairs, feeling a sudden need to see Gran.

Gran's chair was empty.

I tried to stay calm. I didn't usually come home at this time, so maybe she was having her hair done or being taken for a walk. Perhaps she was eating lunch.

Mandy was in the dining-room and asked why I was home so early. I wanted to ask why she wasn't at school herself, but instead I yelled at her.

"Where's Gran? Who's the ambulance for?"

Mandy told me not to shout at her. She said Gran was in her room with Neelam and...I didn't wait to hear the rest, I charged down the corridor to find Gran's room full of people wearing medical-looking uniforms. When Neelam saw me she led me out of the room and shut Gran's door.

"Don't be scared, Billy. Gran's not feeling too good so I called an ambulance just to be on the safe side. But what are you doing here? Why aren't you at school?"

"It's because I was mean to her yesterday isn't it," I said. "It's my fault!"

"Of course it's not your fault," said Neelam, calmly. "I'm sure there's nothing to worry about."

But there *was* something to worry about because a few minutes later, Gran was carried out of her room on a stretcher and taken down in the lift. I didn't even get the chance to speak to her.

I watched the ambulance leave Autumn Days from my window. Everything was going wrong. First the fire flashback at the Safety Centre, the jewellery going missing, Jude's horrible tricks and now Gran going to hospital.

I heard Neelam come in.

"Billy, Gran needs to go somewhere they can look after her properly," she said. "They can make her better in the hospital and then she can come home."

The way she said it made me wonder if I would ever see Gran again.

Eighteen

Russia, nine months ago

After three months of terrifying driving lessons with Jana, and exhausting gym sessions with Izolda, Manya was relieved to be able to catch up on some schoolwork in her room.

A knock on the door made her jump and, with a sinking heart, she went to see what sort of hideous task would be waiting for her. Nobody was in the corridor outside, but a large wicker box had been left with a note attached.

Congratulations, take a break from the gym tonight and enjoy the contents.

She took the box into her room and lifted the lid. Inside were lots of small packages wrapped in white tissue paper. Slowly, Manya started opening the packages and placing them on the floor beside her.

First out was an expensive looking packet of cheese crackers, followed by a wooden container with a selection of French cheeses. Next came a jar of German pâté, some almonds, a bunch of grapes, hard boiled eggs, a large, crusty loaf of bread and a box of Swiss chocolates. Three bottles of different coloured fruit juices had been carefully wrapped and finally, at the very bottom was a flat square box from which a delicious smell was emanating. Manya ripped it open to find the biggest pizza she had ever seen. It was covered with cheese, tomatoes, peppers, tiny sausages and olives.

For three months, Manya had been made to feel insignificant, worthless and more than a little scared. Suddenly she felt valued. Tatiana must be pleased with her. But who could she share the feast with? Dare she invite Feliks?

She didn't stop to think for long in case she changed her mind and ended up eating the food alone. No, this was an evening to celebrate, and she would choose to celebrate with her friend. She quickly downloaded a film on her computer and started playing it with the volume turned high. If Tatiana was trying to listen in, she would think she was watching the film on her own. Leaving her phone on the desk, Manya packed as much of the food as she could into a rucksack and quietly walked out of the girls' boarding house carrying the pizza box.

Standing outside Feliks door she began to have doubts. *Will Feliks be in his room? Will Karine be there? Will he be pleased to see me?*

She raised her arm to knock but hesitated. So many things could go wrong, maybe she should just go back to her room. At that moment the door opened, and Feliks appeared, looking astonished to see her.

"Hello stranger!" he said, smiling broadly. "Are you here to see *me*?"

Manya blushed, but before she could speak Feliks noticed the pizza box.

"If that's for me, you can come in," he said. "If you've come to torment me with it, then you'd better go away. That's the biggest pizza I've ever seen!"

Manya smiled too and went into the room with Feliks. He was alone *and* he was pleased to see her. A comforting warmth crept over her shoulders, and she felt a huge wave of relief.

"Don't you speak anymore?" asked Feliks, giving her a friendly push. He sat on his bed and indicated for Manya to sit on the chair by his desk.

"I suppose I wasn't expecting you to be here," she said, her voice coming out all shaky. "I've got this food, and I thought maybe you'd like to share it?"

"Relax, Manya," said Feliks. "I was about to go to the dining-room, but this looks much better. What's it for?"

Manya hadn't thought up an explanation. She couldn't tell him where it was from.

"My dad sent it for doing well in a test. He's been quite generous recently." It hurt to say it, but she couldn't think of anything else on the spur of the moment.

Manya unpacked the food from the rucksack, and Feliks got a spare sheet out of his cupboard. He laid it out on the floor and together they arranged the picnic. If the pizza had been made of plastic, Manya wouldn't have cared. She felt so at ease, so content with Feliks, and they happily gorged themselves while catching up with each other's news. Karine's name didn't come up once.

Feliks suddenly became serious. "Manya, your dad didn't send this did he? Look, it's not really my business, but you've been my friend for a long time, and I'm looking out for you. The girl who hated games lessons even more than language lessons, suddenly looks like an Olympic athlete. I know you're up to something."

Manya got up to leave. She didn't know how to explain the gym, the driving, the food, any of it. She was scared the film on her laptop might have come to an end and Tatiana would be calling her mobile.

She left the rucksack and the food and ran back to her room. Her phone was lying silent on the table, and the film hadn't even finished. Everything was fine, she could stop worrying.

A message flashed up, making her jump, but it was Feliks.

Be careful. I'm here if you need me. Fx

"Now you're fit enough, we can begin martial arts," said Izolda. "We will start with Judo, then Taekwondo and move onto Karate."

It was the evening after the pizza night, and Manya had not been summoned for driving. She was grateful for a morning off, and hoped the lessons were over. The gym sessions weren't over, that was clear, and she knew nothing about martial arts except that they were a form of self-defence.

Izolda didn't hold back with her kicks and arm-locks during the first session, and Manya felt as though she'd fallen down three flights of stairs by the time she got into bed that night.

The next morning she was woken at 5.00 with a familiar message:

Front gates 5.30am

Manya dragged herself to the school entrance where Jana was waiting for her. It might have been the light, but Manya thought her instructor looked even more grim than usual. When they arrived at the airfield, Jana got out of the car, only this time she didn't swap seats.

"You're moving to advanced driving now with Grusha. You won't see me again."

Manya wasn't sorry to see the back of her driving instructor, but Jana looked like a saint compared with Grusha, an enormous woman with wild grey hair and hands as big as plates who was striding determinedly towards the car.

"We'll begin with emergency stops," said Grusha, heaving herself into the driver's seat. "I demonstrate, you watch."

Grusha drove to a new part of the airfield. A brick wall had been constructed across the road and Grusha accelerated towards it. Manya braced herself, she couldn't believe Grusha would be able to break before hitting the wall. But the woman slammed her feet down on the pedals and the car screeched to a halt, millimetres away from the wall.

Grusha turned the car, drove a distance from the wall and turned it round. She got out of the car, indicating for Manya to take the driver's seat.

"Your turn," she said. "But the spark plugs are misfiring, I need to fix them."

Grusha hurled herself under the car, not seeming to care about the mud on the ground, or the oil smearing her clothes.

Manya waited for Grusha to reappear. She didn't know what spark plugs were for, but she would prefer them to be working before performing her first emergency stop. She started the engine and Grusha put her head through the passenger window.

"I'm going to observe from here," she said. "I don't deal with jellyfish, so make sure to get up a good speed, at least sixty, then leave it until the last minute before breaking hard. I don't want to see more than a metre between the wall and your front bumper when you come to a halt."

Manya had plenty of questions, but Grusha had already retreated and was standing with her arms folded across her massive chest.

The wall was about five hundred metres directly in front, enough distance to pick up a good speed, and Manya revved the engine. She wanted to make a good first impression with her fierce new instructor.

She pressed her foot down on the accelerator and the car sped forwards, quickly reaching forty kilometres an hour, fifty, sixty, seventy. The wall came closer every second, but Manya waited until the last moment before slamming her foot on the brake.

Nothing happened. There was no resistance under her foot, the car didn't even slow down, and Manya screamed as the car ploughed into the wall.

Nineteen

England, the present

I felt scared and worried the whole time Gran was in hospital. The only good thing to come out of it was the proof that she wasn't the Autumn Days thief. More things went missing, and as Gran wasn't there, she couldn't have taken them. Frank's silver bookmark was the next thing to vanish, he was very upset.

"That were a present from me niece," he said. "It were right inside me book, just on that table there. I only went out to get a cuppa. Something fishy's going on, and I reckon I know who's behind it. I just need proof."

I knew Frank thought it was Mandy, but I was certain he was wrong, so I needed to find out the truth before he offended anyone. He'd already told Mandy not to go anywhere near his medals, but luckily she didn't understand what he was talking about. She just shook her head at the ridiculous contraption he'd made to ensure that nobody could prise the medals off his jacket. He'd made it out of card, string and thick tape. The whole thing was safety-pinned and possibly even super-glued.

My first suspect was Beryl. I watched her carefully for an hour on Saturday morning, but she spent the whole time knitting and falling asleep, so it got boring. I sneaked into her room when nobody was looking. Apart from her Spurs calendars there was nothing interesting. I had a quick look in her cupboard, but I drew the line at the drawers, in case she kept her false teeth there. I saw Gran's teeth in a glass of water once. Pink, white and rank, smiling down at me from the shelf. I wrote a great horror story in English the next day called, "Nightmare on the Bathroom Shelf", but I didn't get a very good mark. Mrs Beaman said it was "too far-fetched".

As I was walking back to the lounge, Beryl, came hobbling towards me on her zimmer frame with a gold chain hanging off the handle. It had a gold locket swinging backwards and forwards, a gold locket just like Neelam's.

"What have you got there, Beryl?" I asked, pointing at the locket.

"It's for my friend, Birdie," she said. "It's her birthday and she's going to love this."

Have you taken anything else for your friend?" I asked.

"Yes, lots of things," said Beryl, proudly.

I went back to my room to work out what to do. Beryl wasn't a thief, she was an old lady with dementia and it could be that her dementia *made* her steal things. I couldn't be the one to tell on Beryl. What if she got into trouble? So many people don't understand dementia. Don't understand that it makes people do things they would never have done before. True, she was embarrassing a lot of the time, but underneath she was a good person.

I would have to find a way to return all the missing stuff without anyone finding out.

Louis came back on Saturday afternoon. He was worried about Gran and about me being worried about Gran. He asked if I wanted to play football in the park. I did.

After running about until we could hardly breathe, we went to sit on a bench overlooking the lake.

"Do you think Gran's coming home soon?" I asked.

"Billy, your Gran is very old, and she's had a tough few years, but despite what she's been through she's always cheerful. So many old people are grumpy and negative, but Gran is a lot of fun. That poor brain of hers is like a maze. She keeps losing her way and coming to a dead end. It's very confusing for her not being able to remember things. Maybe she'll come back from hospital as right as rain, but whatever happens, you know you'll always have me and Neelam."

"Do you think Gran might not come back?" I asked, my hands suddenly feeling clammy and my mouth all dry.

"Come on Billy, we've got to be positive. It's no good worrying about things we have no control over. I expect Gran will be back at Autumn Days very soon, smiling and talking in that funny way of hers."

"But she's the only real family I've got. If she's not there, where will I go?" I asked, adding heart palpitations to my symptoms.

"Billy, that's not true, we're *all* your family. Me, Neelam, Frank, Pascal, Beryl, Mary and even Mandy. I told you before, Neelam signed special papers which make her your guardian. She's responsible for you, just like a parent would be. After the fire the authorities wanted to find a foster mum for you, someone who would take you to live in their house, but Neelam insisted you must stay with Gran and she promised to look after you until your parents came for you."

"But they haven't come for me have they," I said.

"Not yet, but nobody knows what happened to them on the night of the fire, so you mustn't give up hope. And in the meantime, you'll just have to make do with me and Neelam. And I s'pose Neelam and I will have to put up with you," he added with a grin on his face.

He stood up and threw the football to me.

"Let's go back for tea," he said. "I could eat a whole cake!"

"Can you tell me what happened the night of the fire?" I asked when we got back to Autumn Days.

"But Billy, I've told you that story a hundred times, you must know it off by heart."

"Yes, but I'm looking at it from a different angle now. There might be some details you've missed."

"You've been working on this new theory have you?" said Louis, taking an enormous bite of Mandy's honey cake and licking his fingers.

"It's not going very well," I said. "I need to speak to someone, but I don't know where to find them."

"Can I help?"

"Maybe, but I have a few ideas to try out first. What did you see when you arrived at the house?"

"The fire had taken hold quickly, and we could see the glow from quite a distance in the darkness. Paul and I grabbed the hose and ran towards the house. The front door was locked, so we had to smash it down."

"So the door was definitely shut?"

"Definitely. The hall was full of flames and the smoke was so thick we could hardly see. We were wearing oxygen masks and I was using our thermal imaging camera which shows people hidden in the smoke."

"And that's when you found Gran?"

"That's right, she was holding onto a chair and I remember picking her up and carrying her out into the fresh air. She was coughing, but thankfully didn't seem to have any burns. I heard the Watch Commander yelling into his radio, asking for more pumps.

"I left Gran with the paramedics and ran back to the front door with the Watch Commander shouting after me, "Two minutes! I want you out in two minutes!"

"Why did you only have two minutes?"

"The Watch Commander has to judge how long it is before a building becomes too dangerous."

"You only had two minutes and I was still in there?"

"Is this too much detail?" asked Louis. "I don't want you having nightmares."

"No, I want you to tell me everything. Please Louis, it's really important."

"Okay, but stop me if it's too much."

I nodded. There was no way I was going to stop him. He'd never given me this much detail before.

"Paul and I edged our way up the stairs together. That's what you have to do, work together. But the fire was spreading, and we knew we had to be quick. We checked the bedrooms and they were all empty apart from one."

"So my parents weren't in the house?"

"No. And we had to make a report afterwards to say that we checked thoroughly because nobody knew where your parents could have got to."

"They were kidnapped!" I said, the words blurting out by mistake.

I was expecting Louis to laugh, but he looked at me seriously.

"To be perfectly honest, Billy, I think you have a point. It's not my place to say anything, and I know the police have been investigating the case for years, but I don't understand why they're not making any headway."

"That's why I'm having to look into it myself."

"And I reckon I'd do the same thing in your position. Neelam's always asking if there's been a breakthrough."

"Wasn't there *anyone* who knew my parents?"

"Apparently not. The neighbours said your family had moved in that same day."

"Surely the person who sold them the house would have had their details?"

"They rented the house under fake names."

"What! Fake names? Louis, why haven't you told me this before?"

"You were so little at the time. Neelam and I thought it was better not to scare you."

"Why would my parents use fake names?"

"Possibly they were hiding from someone?"

All this new information was baffling. Part of me was thrilled with the intrigue of it all, but at the same time I was struggling not to be furious with Neelam and Louis for not telling me all this before.

"What else haven't you told me?" I asked. "I had a flashback at the Safety Centre. I remember you carrying me out."

"You remember that? You were such a tiny little boy, just standing on your bed in your pyjamas, holding your teddy and looking at me with big, scared eyes."

"And then there was an explosion," I said.

"You're right," said Louis looking down.

"And you're not telling me something, I can tell. What was the explosion?"

Louis sighed. "I s'pose you have a right to know, mate."

I waited while Louis got his thoughts in order. I could tell it was a big deal for him and he felt uncomfortable about what he was going to tell me.

"After we'd made sure there was nobody else in the house, I ran round the back and I saw the back door was open."

"Do you think my parents had run out of the house?" I said, aghast. Surely they wouldn't have left me and Gran to burn in the fire.

"No! No, Billy, that's not what I'm saying at all. What I'm trying to tell you, and I'm not doing it very well, is that someone had broken in through the back door."

"Are you sure?"

"That explosion you heard was caused by three gas canisters. We found them after the fire had been put out."

Someone had broken into our house, set fire to it and left gas canisters to make quite sure nothing was left.

"They tried to kill us?" I whispered.

Louis took my shoulders. "Listen mate, you're okay. Gran's okay. You're safe here."

"But Mum and Dad aren't okay are they!" I said, my skin was crawling, my blood felt close to boiling point. "Why hasn't anyone done anything about that?"

"I don't know," said Louis, quietly. "I'd like to help you, Billy. I just don't know what more I can do."

"Is there anything else you've forgotten to tell me," I said, trying not to let my emotions spill out.

"Yes, actually, there is one more thing; how strange to remember it now. It was when I was carrying you out to the ambulance. There was a little girl sitting on the curb near the house, all by herself. What on earth was she doing there?"

Before I could ask Louis anything about the girl, there was a shout from the kitchen. It sounded like, "Moya zevenet!"

It was Mandy running out of the kitchen shaking her hand as though she'd burnt it. She raced round the room, checking everyone's fingers, looking under all the cushions, searching the floor.

"Babushka's ring, Babushka's ring," she kept saying.

Frank came over and spoke in a low voice. "She's faking this," he said. "I reckon she's the one who's been stealing everything and now she's pretending something of hers has gone to avert suspicion. Seen it all the time in me army days."

Louis looked at his watch. "Oh my days, I'm on duty! Sorry Billy, I have to go." He bent down to pick up his wallet. "Hang on a minute," he said. "Where are my keys?"

Twenty
Russia, nine months ago

In the split second between the brakes not engaging and the car hitting the wall, Manya shut her eyes tightly and prayed the car had been fitted with an airbag. In her head she could see flames, feel the heat of a fire and hear a woman's voice, "No! My little boy is in the house!"

The impact never came. There was a huge ripping sound, and Manya was aware that the car was still moving forwards at speed. She opened her eyes to see a clear runway in front of her. With one hand back on the steering wheel and the other pulling the handbrake, she regained control of the car and brought it to a halt.

Manya sat in the car for a long time. In the rear-view mirror she could see the remains of the paper wall. It had looked so realistic from the other side, even close-up. Grusha was nowhere to be seen, and Manya knew now that she hadn't been fixing the spark plugs at all. She'd been cutting the brakes.

Remembering the grim look on Jana's face, Manya suspected she and Tatiana had organised the whole thing. Were they trying to scare her just because she'd shared her food with Feliks?

Still shaking, she climbed out of the car and walked back to the wall. Most of the paper was in shreds, but standing on the other side of the wall she could see why she'd been fooled. Part of the structure remained standing, supported by thin metal rods. It was certainly a clever illusion.

Making her way to the entrance of the airfield, Manya began the long walk back to school. According to her phone it should take just under two hours. At least it would give her time to think about what had just happened. There was a lot to process.

The first thing to contemplate was why an image of flames had come into her head as the car hit the fake wall. Somehow she knew a memory was deeply entrenched in her mind, but no matter how hard she concentrated, she couldn't bring it forward. A woman crying for her little boy, and everything feeling hot. Could it have been the terror of the broken brakes throwing up strange ideas, or was she remembering a bad dream? No, something was telling her the flames and the voice were real.

On the final stretch of road to school, Manya sensed a car pulling up beside her. Tatiana was at the wheel, and even though Manya had plenty of questions, she wasn't in the right frame of mind to talk to her right now so she carried on walking. Tatiana pressed the horn, but Manya ignored her. Tatiana drew up next to Manya again and drove slowly alongside while pressing her hand continuously on the horn. The noise was causing confusion amongst the other motorists and people were beginning to stare. Manya opened the car door, ready to tell

Tatiana to leave her alone, when she saw a gun. Tatiana stopped pressing the horn and pointed the revolver at Manya.

"Get in," she said.

Two hours later, Manya found herself in the bedroom of a large apartment, surrounded by her belongings. Tatiana had somehow signed her out of school, thrown everything haphazardly into plastic bags, and transferred it to the car while Manya had been facing her ordeal with Grusha.

In her new room, Manya sat on the bed. If only she had asked for Feliks's help, maybe none of this would have happened. Was it too late to send him a message and for him to come and find her? Of course, her phone had gone, Tatiana had had ample opportunity to take it. She lay back on the bed, too scared and too tired to work out what to do next.

Tatiana entered the room. "You might as well unpack," she said. "This will be your home for the next month."

"What if I don't want to carry on?" said Manya, defiantly, determined not to let Tatiana see how frightened she was.

"You don't have a choice," said Tatiana. "You were supposed to remain in your room, but your stupid attempt to deceive us last night was a mistake. Your pacifist friend has far too much influence over you, and we can't take any chances. We've invested time and money in your training, Manya. You're committed to the cause now, whether you like it or not."

Tatiana started to walk out of the room, but paused before adding, "And remember, next time the wall might not be made of paper."

Izolda arrived early the following morning, and the martial arts training continued, along with a rigorous training schedule to keep up Manya's fitness levels.

There was no more driving, but when Izolda left at lunch time every day, a homely looking woman called Galina arrived.

"Can you cook?" she asked, on her first visit.

"A little," said Manya. "My grandmother taught me how to bake."

"That's a very good start," said Galina kindly. "In that case we will begin by enhancing your baking skills, and then we will move to British cooking. My task is to teach you to cook just like the English."

"But why?" asked Manya.

"I've no idea," said Galina. " I'm just obeying orders."

"I thought English people only ate roast beef or fish and chips," said Manya.

Galina laughed. "I think we can find a few other dishes," she said. "I've been assigned a very specific task. You are to learn how to cook for elderly British citizens living in an old people's home."

The flames were engulfing the house and the woman was crying, "My little boy!" over and over. Manya tried to save the child, but she was too late.

She woke up sweating. It was the same nightmare every night, ever since the incident with the broken brakes, but Manya couldn't find the answer; even looking up what it meant to dream about fire, but nothing made sense. She was convinced something real had happened to her, something she'd forgotten.

A month later, Manya found herself on a plane heading towards England. She had a new passport and a new driving licence, both stamped with the name Mandy Surkova.

She was heading for a care home called Autumn Days where she would help with cooking and baking. Tatiana had organised the position, and Neelam, the care home manager, had said she would be able to live on site in the staff accommodation.

Tatiana had given Manya the task of enrolling herself in the local school. "Hacking into school systems is your speciality," she said. "You shouldn't have much trouble getting your name onto the system."

"Why do I need to go to school?" asked Manya.

"You will be given the full details of the assignment once you are in England. Just get yourself into the school," said Tatiana.

If Manya had known she would be going to England, she would have worked on her spoken English. English language was one of the many subjects she had dropped in favour of furthering her IT skills. She knew plenty of technological terms such as 'encryption', 'phishing', and 'cybersecurity', but when it came to everyday useful conversation she was lacking even in the basics.

At the airport, she had bought an English phrase book and opened the book at the 'Useful Phrases' chapter.

Thanks so much, I really appreciate it.

Actually, I'm running a bit behind.

Fancy a cuppa?

Manya couldn't imagine an occasion when she could use these phrases, but then she had no idea what British people were like. Her only recollection from school was that British people drank tea with milk at five o'clock every day, they invented sports which Russian people beat them at, and men wore skirts.

A year ago, Manya would have been terrified about moving to a foreign country, but having spent a month sleeping in an apartment with Tatiana, and quite probably Tatiana's gun, in the next room, it was a relief to be getting away.

Manya didn't remember flying before, but entering the aircraft she had a sense of déjà vu. Maybe her parents had flown somewhere with her when she was little. It would have been helpful to ask her father, but it was another of Tatiana's conditions that there was to be no contact with anyone in Russia once Manya was in England. Even messages to Tatiana herself would be restricted.

"You are to get on with the assignment and not ask questions," Tatiana had said. "Your father knows why you won't be contactable for the foreseeable future. He believes you've been fast-tracked at Kolmogorov, and you're involved in some top-secret research at the university. He says he's proud of you."

Manya doubted her father would be proud of her. But more than that, she was puzzled as to why Tatiana would be in touch with him.

Twenty-One

England, the present

"Seriously, Neelam," said Louis. "My shift begins in an hour, I need my keys!"

I wasn't entirely sure what to do. I knew Beryl was the thief, but I'd wanted to have a quiet chat with her, not outright accuse her.

Neelam was asking all the residents if they'd seen the keys, but Louis was getting impatient.

"I'm going to have to check the rooms, Neelam," he said. "I know it's against the regulations and everything, but this is an emergency."

"Okay," Neelam said, hesitantly. "Take Billy, and don't touch anything."

Maybe it was for the best. This way, Beryl's kleptomaniac tendencies would be uncovered without me dobbing her in. Louis would know what to do.

As we walked towards Beryl's room, a wailing sound drifted towards us. It was Beryl. She was singing.

"Come here Birdie-Birdie," she sang. "I've got you a present. Come here my little one." There was a jangling sound.

Louis and I exchanged glances and entered the room. Beryl was leaning out through the open window and didn't notice us. A big magpie flew down, perched on the windowsill and Beryl handed him a bunch of keys. Louis's keys.

"There you go, Birdie. Happy birthday," sang Beryl as the magpie flew off with the keys. Louis disappeared, calling back, "Don't let her fall out!"

"Beryl," I said, going to stand next to her at the window. "Have you made a friend?"

"Ooh yes, that's Birdie, he loves shiny things. I give him presents and he takes them to his nest over there in that tree. Have you got anything shiny?"

Through the window I could see Louis searching on the ground, but the magpie was sitting on a branch with the keys in its beak. Maybe they were too heavy, maybe they weren't shiny enough, but suddenly, the magpie dropped Louis's keys. They fell to the branch below and got stuck on a twig.

"You'll need a ladder," I called down to Louis.

"I haven't got time for that," he shouted back, running towards the tree. He took a massive jump and held onto the branch with both hands. Then he sort of walked up the tree trunk, grabbed his keys and dropped down to the grass.

"Gotta go. See you mate," he shouted. Then he was gone.

I looked at Beryl who'd been watching too.

"Blimey," she said. "What a dish!"

It turned out that all the missing items had been taken by Beryl to give to the magpie. All the watches, jewellery, Pascal's tie pin, Frank's bookmark and Mandy's ring. The gardener came round, put a long ladder up the tree and found all the missing things near the magpie's nest.

That time when Gran picked up Beryl's bracelet in the garden was because Beryl had given it to the magpie who'd then dropped it onto the bush and Gran had picked it up.

I thought it was funny, and I was relieved Beryl wasn't a real thief, but Beryl was cross when Neelam kept checking up on her. "Don't keep asking me if I've taken anything that's not mine. I would never do such a thing!" she said every time.

Katie was back at school on Monday. I couldn't wait to tell her about Jude's dad and my conspiracy theory. Now that I knew for sure my parents had been kidnapped, it all felt very real and scary. I couldn't get the idea of the gas canisters out of my head. Jude was bad, but could his dad really have been so evil as to blow up the house without checking whether there was anyone in it? There was only one way to find out.

"Let's follow Jude after school and see if his dad's there," said Katie. "We've got to find out what he looks like."

"We don't need to follow him, I know where he lives," I said.

As soon as the last lesson finished, we ran to the park where the man with the violin had moved his cup to a new position, right next to his foot. I showed Katie the narrow alleyway and the route Jude had taken to get home. I had a little trouble remembering which house was Jude's, but then I remembered the brown tape on the window.

"I'll ring the bell, see if anyone's at home," said Katie.

"What are you going to say?"

"I don't know, but I'll think of something," she said.

I kept a lookout for Jude while Katie rang the doorbell. I wasn't expecting anyone to answer, but a large woman, wearing a fluorescent green dressing-gown and a pink towel wrapped around her head, came to the door with a cigarette in her mouth.

"Er, is Jude home yet?" I heard Katie ask.

"You 'is girlfriend or what?" said the woman.

"I wanted to speak to Mr Doyle," said Katie. "Is he here?"

"Are ya jokin'. Clear off." She slammed the door in Katie's face, but I could see her peeping out of a window from behind a torn curtain.

Katie was furious. "I wasn't being rude, was I? She didn't need to be so aggressive. D'you think that was Jude's mum?"

"I don't know," I said. "But let's go before he gets home."

On reflection, it wasn't very clever to take the same route. Not when Jude was on his way home. We were halfway back up the alleyway when he appeared, and he wasn't alone. Tyrone was walking next to Jude, they both had their heads down, and Big Ben was right behind, towering over them like a gormless troll.

Big Ben saw us first, but it took a couple of seconds for him to register.

"Dude, Dude," he stammered, with a lot of bacon roll spilling out of his mouth. He tried to push past the others and knocked them both into the fence.

"Keep walking," said Katie. "They're not going to do anything to us."

I wasn't sure of Katie's reasoning at this point, especially when Jude and Tyrone both yelled together, "Get them!"

I grabbed Katie's arm and we shot back down the alleyway with the three boys pounding after us.

But then the strangest thing happened: the footsteps stopped.

"Where are they?" I said.

"I bet they're waiting in the footpath, ready to jump on us if we go back," said Katie.

Having seen the look on Jude's face, it wouldn't have been sensible to go back into the alleyway, so we found a different route. Katie was late for her water polo match and I was going to miss the cakes if I didn't get going.

When I got home, Neelam was waiting for me.

"Where've you been, Billy?" she asked. "It's nearly dark and I was getting worried. I thought something bad must have happened with Mandy missing too."

"I wasn't with Mandy, I was with Katie. We just got, erm, caught up with something."

Just then, Mandy came limping down the corridor.

"Is everything okay, Mandy?" asked Neelam. "Billy was late too, and I thought there might have been an accident."

"Not accident," said Mandy. She seemed cross.

"What happened to your leg?" asked Neelam.

"My foot made connection with some, how to say, garbage?"

The following morning Jude and the gang came to school covered with cuts and bruises.

"Do you think they fell over each other?" Katie suggested.

It was a mystery which hadn't brought us any closer to finding Mr Doyle. I knew the next step was to speak to him, but if Jude didn't live with his dad, it was going to be even more difficult to find him. Katie said she had a few ideas, so I invited her to come to Autumn Days on Saturday. I hoped Gran would be home by then.

Twenty-Two

England, six months ago

The pilot announced the plane would be landing in fifteen minutes, and Manya looked out of the window at the patchwork of green fields below. It didn't appear to be raining, which was strange because it was supposed to rain constantly in England.

Neelam had driven to the airport to collect Manya. If she was surprised at her lack of English, she didn't show it, but chatted casually about Autumn Days, the residents and what would be required of her. Manya couldn't understand much, and struggled to concentrate. She was eager to charge up her new laptop and discover the important assignment she'd been given. The assignment that would make Russia proud of her.

Autumn Days was a large, imposing building from the outside, but the interior was welcoming, with music playing, staff bustling and old people sitting in groups of four, playing card games. Neelam led Manya to the lift and they came out into another lounge.

"Ooh hello lovely," called a lady with dyed red hair who was sitting near the lift. "She's a bit young for this place isn't she, Neelam? Has she lost her marbles already?"

"Take no notice of Beryl," said Neelam quietly, before announcing, "If I could have your attention for a moment everyone? I'd like you all to meet Mandy, she's our new chef. Apparently she makes excellent cakes."

There was a whoop from one old man and a smattering of applause from the others who'd been listening.

"Hallo," she said, "I happy to meeting you today."

One of the men muttered something under his breath, but Manya didn't understand the term, "blumin foreigners".

"Please I go in my room for taking my bags?" she said, turning to Neelam, desperate to get into her laptop.

Neelam showed her to a single room with a wash basin, a large cupboard, a bed and a chest of drawers which doubled as a desk. The moment she was alone, Manya took out her laptop and plugged it in with the special three-pronged plug Tatiana had given her. It flickered to life and Manya entered the code to open the secret link. She held her breath and started to read.

Open the next section when you are alone. The file will be available for five minutes, then it will self-delete.

Manya clicked on the link and another page appeared.

1. *Locate Billy, Autumn Days resident.*

2. *Keep close to Billy.*

3. *Photos of Billy to be taken discreetly and forwarded to Tatiana every month.*

4. *Billy is a target, so always be wary of suspicious vehicles or people who could be following him.*

5. *Your cover is cook at Autumn Days. You will receive a small payment for this.* ***Never*** *reveal your true identity.*

6. *Contact Tatiana only in an emergency.*

7. ***DO NOT*** *contact anyone in Russia, including your parents.*

Was that it? Who was this old man Billy? Why was he so special? There must be another document, thought Manya, desperately looking for something more.

There was nothing.

Manya sat on her bed feeling puzzled and let-down. In what way would her computer skills, that she'd worked on so diligently, be needed simply to take photos? What was all the driving and self-defence for, and why was Billy a target? Surely she needed to know who was targeting him.

Looking out of the window at the strange world outside, Manya suddenly felt very young and alone, thousands of miles away from home in a country where she didn't speak the language. Was she really supposed to be cooking for old people who looked as though they wouldn't know the difference between seafood and cat food?

There was a knock at the door, and she stood up to open it, expecting to see Neelam. A boy was standing in the doorway.

"Hi, I'm Billy," he said. "I've just got home from school, and I thought I'd introduce myself."

So this was Billy, not an old man after all. Did he live here in the old people's home, and need protecting? Did he *know* he needed protecting?

Manya began to console herself with the thought that at least there was some sort of mystery to solve.

"Come, Billy," said Manya. "I Mandy, and I come England for job cooking. I make food for old people."

"I know," said Billy. "Neelam told me."

"Why you live here?" asked Manya.

Billy, who'd been looking around the room, especially at the laptop on the desk, turned to face her, but he didn't answer her question. Instead he began a barrage of his own: why was she in England, where were her parents, how good was her English, what was school like in Russia, did she have any good games on her laptop, could he borrow her laptop sometimes, which football team did she support?

Manya answered as well as she could, but after about ten minutes Billy stood up and said he needed to talk to Gran. Manya was left with a feeling that she'd been the one to have been interrogated.

She'd discovered absolutely nothing about the boy she was here to protect.

That night, the fire dream returned, this time it was even more vivid. Manya was in a parked car. She'd been sleeping on the back seat and now she sat up to look around, trying to work out where she was. It was dark, except for a red glow rising up from somewhere ahead. She fumbled for the door handle and climbed out of the car, to find a blazing house, from which the intense heat could be felt, even from a distance.

Suddenly two men and a woman appeared. The men were grappling with the screaming woman, dragging her away from the house...

Manya woke up sweating, trying to remember what came after the screaming, but the dream slipped away again. Why did she keep having this dream and why did it feel so real?

It was impossible to get back to sleep, with so many questions whirring around her head, and Manya was relieved when a dim grey light appeared around the edges of the curtains. She got out of bed, determined to find out everything she could about Billy.

But Neelam had a different agenda, which meant Manya was busy all day. Gordon, the head cook, showed her around the kitchen and gave her a full run-down of the timetable. She worked alongside him as he prepared the meals for the day, and by lunchtime she'd learnt new English phrases such as 'whisk this one up a treat', 'flip it over', and 'we don't want to end up with a soggy bottom'.

Neelam introduced her properly to the residents, but she struggled to understand them, especially a bandana-wearing man called Pasqual, who closed his eyes when he spoke and twirled his fingers. She had the feeling she was being scrutinised by Beryl, and Frank wouldn't speak to her at all. The only person she felt drawn towards was called Gran, the lady with the doll, whose smile and twinkling eyes reminded her of Babushka.

There was no opportunity to ask Neelam about Billy and anyway, she needed to be careful. In Neelam's eyes she was here to cook, she mustn't appear too interested in Billy.

By the end of the first day, she was exhausted, but determined to discover more the following day at Billy's school.

There had been no problem enrolling at the school. The system had been easy to hack into, and Manya simply added her name to the sixth-form list. Sixth formers didn't wear a uniform, all she needed was a lanyard showing identification. She'd copied the school badge onto a small white card and filled in her details. There were so many pupils in the school, nobody would notice her if she was careful.

English school, on the surface, didn't seem particularly different from the Russian schools she was used to. Children arrived in groups making lots of noise, disappeared for lessons, then reappeared for breaks, making lots more noise. The one big difference was the lack of patriotism. At her schools, the Russian flag had always been on display and an extra-large one would be hauled up the flagpole on special occasions. At Billy's school there were no British flags to be seen anywhere.

As the days passed, Manya grew more and more frustrated. Neelam never had time to talk to her and anyway, Manya had a feeling she wouldn't readily share anything confidential, so she needed to find a way to get information from Billy himself. Then there were the photos which were surprisingly difficult to take discreetly.

After a few days of making no headway, Manya stood by the school gates at the end of the day, waiting for Billy to come out. She pretended to be surprised to see him.

"Billy!" she said.

"Oh, Mandy," he replied, not looking thrilled to see her. "What are you doing here?"

"I go home now. We walk together, yes?"

"I didn't know you were in England to go to school. Is it some sort of work-study scheme? Is that what you do in Russia?"

How did this boy always turn it around so he was the one asking the questions? They were nearly halfway home; Manya needed to move things forward.

"Why you live in home with old people?"

"Actually, nobody knows I live there, it's a secret, okay?"

This was better, Billy was living at Autumn Days secretly. Perhaps he knew who he was hiding from.

"I understand," said Manya. "I not let you have danger."

"Danger? I'm not in danger, I just don't want people at school to know. It's embarrassing."

Billy ran ahead, leaving Manya even more mystified than ever.

Twenty-Three

England, the present

On Wednesday, Gran was well enough for visitors, so Neelam took me after school.

The hospital was enormous and grey and miserable. There were lots of ill-looking people walking very slowly, tired-looking doctors with clip-boards and worried-looking visitors with flowers wrapped in paper cones. It was horrible.

Neelam led me inside, up stairs and along corridors where patients were lying on beds with wheels. The smell was a mixture of medicine, over-cooked food and disinfectant: no wonder people were ill. Eventually we arrived at a big room with blue curtains hanging down from the ceiling, where nurses smiled at me and old ladies sitting up in narrow beds with metal sides stared at me with empty eyes. Gran shouldn't be in this place where everyone had flat hair and grey skin.

Neelam led me to a bed where a thin colourless old lady lay with her eyes shut. "Look who I've brought to see you," she said. The old lady opened one eye and then shut it again. Was that Gran? Surely not. Gran has bouncy hair, pink cheeks, bright, smiley eyes and she chats all the time. This lady was grey, dull and floppy.

It *was* Gran.

Neelam started telling Gran all the Autumn Days news, but I noticed she didn't mention Beryl or the magpie. I sat on the chair next to the bed.

"Billy, don't you want to say hello to Gran?" she asked.

"What can I say?"

"How about you give her some apple?" Neelam brought out a little jar of apple sauce. She showed me how to scoop some onto the spoon and slide it into Gran's mouth. Gran seemed to know it was good for her, but kept her eyes shut as she swallowed. I managed to get most of it in when she slowly opened her eyes, looked at me, and said in a croaky voice, "Ah Michael, there you are. You're a good boy."

"Hello Gran," I said, "I wish you'd get better soon because we miss you at Autumn Days and I don't think it's very nice here. And you need to get your hair done." That last bit slipped out by accident, and I glanced at Neelam to see if she was cross, but she was smiling and nodding her head at me.

"Also, Gran, when I come home from school, and I look at your empty chair it makes me sad. Please come home. Please try to get better."

I reached into my rucksack, brought out Dardar and handed her to Gran who carefully took the doll and gave it a gentle hug. Then she spoke to Dardar in a tiny voice that I could only just hear,

"That's my son, Michael. He's taking us to the theatre tonight."

Gran arrived home on Friday, and Katie came on Saturday. I introduced her to all the Oldies. Frank was in a good mood and told us a funny story about one of the soldiers in his squad.

"We was all lined up with our uniforms lookin' spick 'n' span. Our hair all tidy, our nails clean and our boots shiny. One poor bloke, Pete his name was, well he hadn't polished his boots enough. There was this tiny speck o'dust on his right foot. That old sergeant went ballistic! Shouted and spat somethin' terrible. He told Pete he wasn't good enough and even though it was his afternoon off, he was going to get punished. D'you know what he had to do? It was a beautiful afternoon, but Pete was made to climb up onto the roof of our shed with a broom to sweep all the sunshine off it! All the sunshine! How was he supposed to sweep sunshine off a shed? There wasn't a cloud in the sky and there he was brushin' and brushin'! Couldn't come down till eight o' clock when the sun set. You can bet Pete had the shiniest boots in the whole platoon after that! He never wanted to brush sunshine again!"

Katie thought Frank's story was hilarious and of course, Frank loved that. He stood up and did a little dance around his chair which made Katie laugh even more. She didn't flinch at all when she saw Mary's poor twisted face, and she had a chat with Gran.

"Hello, I'm Billy's friend Katie," said Katie.

"How lovely," said Gran. "Who's Billy?"

"Billy's got a girlfriend," sang Beryl from the other side of the room. I smiled an apology to Katie, and we went to my room to get on with our investigations without being interrupted. Katie had brought her laptop and said we should start by trying to find more about Mr Doyle.

"We just need to dig around a bit; we should be able to find him on LinkedIn," she said. "Or X. My dad uses them to find businesspeople all the time."

It didn't take long to find a photo of Patrick Doyle, CEO of Doyle Housing.

"He looks too young," I said.

"Don't take any notice of the age," said Katie. "Everyone puts up photos of when they were younger. My dad uses one from about twenty years ago. He doesn't look anything like it now."

"I can't see that man ever being married to the woman we saw at Jude's house," I said. "He's wearing a tie!"

"Can you imagine *anyone* marrying her?" asked Katie.

We tried to find out as much as possible about Patrick Doyle, but the only information was to do with business. We both took a long look at the photo again to remember the face. I didn't think Patrick Doyle looked anything like Jude, but I didn't tell Katie, who was stoked at finding him in the first place. We decided there wasn't much more we could do until we saw Jude on Monday. We'd ask what his dad's name was, and that would be a massive step forward.

Katie said *she* should be the one to ask Jude his dad's name under the circumstances, and we positioned ourselves next to him in the lunch queue.

"Hey Jude," she said casually. " I think I saw a photo of your dad in the paper at the weekend. Something about a building project. What's his first name?"

Jude smirked. "Ah, it's the moron's girlfriend chatting me up," he said. "Have you had enough of him already?"

"Forget it," said Katie. "It was a simple question. I just wondered if it was your dad. Is his name Patrick?"

"Hat-trick?" said Jude, laughing idiotically. "That should be *my* name! Guys, I want you to call me Hat-trick Doyle from now on."

Tyrone laughed. "So, Hat-trick Doyle, you coming round mine tonight?"

Jude looked disappointed. "Can't tonight," he said. "Gotta go to Dad's."

A clue! Jude was going to his dad's, which meant one of two things. Either Jude would be walking to his dad's house after school, or his dad would be picking him up. Whichever it was, I was going to be right behind him.

Twenty-Four

England, one month ago

Manya was getting bored. She'd fulfilled her task of sending photos of Billy every month, but Tatiana refused to tell her why it was necessary. There hardly seemed a reason to protect him and anyway, she didn't know what she was protecting him from. Billy was friendly, but he didn't want to be friends with her. It might be that Frank was so distrustful of her. Did Frank suspect something, or was he simply prejudiced against all foreigners?

She was ready for action. All her training seemed like a waste of time. She hadn't needed her fitness and she hadn't needed to drive once since being in England.

Walking down the corridor to her school locker where she kept nothing but a map of the school, she decided to tell Tatiana she was coming home. It was true she'd grown quite fond of some of the 'Oldies', especially Gran, but it would be better for her to get back to Kolmogorov to finish her studies than spend most of her time baking cakes in the kitchen of a care home.

Two boys were standing by the lockers, one of them had retrieved a large packet of crisps and was cramming them into his mouth.

"This is gonna be good, Ty," he said. "You need a new punchbag dontcha Ty?"

The other boy nodded his head and laughed. "A new punchbag, that's right Benny Boy," and he started dancing on his feet and pummelling the air. "D'ya think Billy's gonna put up more of a fight than the other drips? 'Cos I need a bit more gucci, know what I mean?"

Manya understood very little of the conversation, but she recognised the aggressive body-language and her ears pricked up at the name, 'Billy'. When Tatiana had said Billy was a target, she thought she would be protecting him from some criminal under-cover agency, not a couple of schoolboys. Well, at least she might see some action for a change.

A third boy joined the other two and winked at them. "Tomorrow, after the trip," was all he said.

That evening, Manya overheard Billy talking about his trip to Bletchley Park the following day. It wouldn't be possible for Manya to join him on the coach, but she would certainly be waiting when it arrived back. "Tomorrow after the trip," was what the boy with the blond spiky hair had said.

Not wanting to miss the return of the coach, Manya was waiting in the car park long before the end of the school day, wearing a pair of black jeans and a black hoodie. Simple common sense told her to be as invisible as possible and to be ready for whatever the three boys had planned for Billy.

It was a long wait. Most of the rest of the school had already left, and it was beginning to get dark before the coach finally pulled into the car park in the drizzling rain. As the children piled off the coach, Manya easily distinguished the three boys she'd seen by the lockers, but Billy wasn't so easy to spot.

Finally, there he was, jumping down and striding towards the school gates. But instead of turning right, he turned left. Where could he be going?

As expected, the three other boys followed Billy, left out of the gate, and Manya crept stealthily behind them. The rain was harder now and it was quite dark, making it easy for Manya to remain invisible. However, now it became more difficult to see Billy ahead of the boys.

At the side of the pavement, railings offered a convenient foothold and Manya climbed up to get a better view. Billy had stopped and turned round to face the boys. She couldn't hear what was being said, but instinctively jumped down and dashed past the boys just in time to grab him as he stepped into the road in front of a lorry. In one swift movement she spun Billy away from the road, threw him into a bush and whipped her foot up, taekwondo style, catching one of the boys around the back of the head, making him cry out.

"Chto vy delayete?" she growled fiercely in Russian. "What are you doing?"

Disappointingly, that was all it took. The terrified boys ran off and Manya slipped out of sight before Billy had time to haul himself out of the bush.

It hadn't been the mission she'd been hoping for, but Manya's job suddenly became more interesting. It was almost as though Billy was going out of his way to look for trouble.

One afternoon, for some bizarre reason, Billy had chosen to investigate the leader of the gang. Even more bizarre was the fact that he took his new friend Katie with him. The two of them had a close shave in an alleyway and, if Manya hadn't intervened, Billy would have had more than a telling off from Neelam for being late. Those boys fought dirty and Manya sustained a slight injury when her right foot made contact with Tyrone's backside.

Twenty-Five

England, the present

It was Jiu-Jitsu night for Katie, so I would have to spy on Jude by myself. After the near miss in the alleyway I wasn't thrilled about going alone, but this was an essential mission, an opportunity, at last, to see the face of Jude's dad.

Jude rushed out of the classroom at the end of the day, and I was right behind. He stopped in the car park and I had to pretend to be doing up my shoelaces. Nobody came for him and I was far too conspicuous, so I pretended to have forgotten something, turned back towards the classroom and collided with Mandy.

"Why are you always following me?" I said, wondering if Frank was right after all about her.

Mandy looked surprisingly annoyed and opened her mouth to speak, but a raucous hooting sound made us both turn towards the car park.

An enormous Rolls Royce pulled up next to Jude who leapt in, probably hoping nobody was watching. He had good reason, the car was hideous! The body was bright purple, the bonnet and wheel trims were gold, and it had silver lettering printed along the side of the car: 'Doyle's Cleaning Co."

Was that Jude's dad? The driver was wearing a cap and sunglasses, so it was impossible to tell if he was the Patrick Doyle Katie had found on the website. A woman with long hair, also wearing sunglasses was in the passenger seat. Considering it was winter and nearly dark, the shades were unnecessary, but totally in keeping with the ridiculous car.

The driver revved the engine and swerved around the car park, and as it did, Mandy made a lunge for me as though she thought I was about to get run over.

"What was that for?" I asked.

"You asking me?" she replied as though it was *me* who'd done something wrong. "Why you finding always trouble with bad boy?" she said. "Why you follow him?"

"Well if you must know," I said, getting angry. How did she know I'd been following Jude? Had she been spying on me? "If you must know, it's because I think his dad kidnapped my parents!"

"Your parents?"

That shut her up. "Yes Mandy. That man in the car burnt down our house and that's why I live in a care home with lots of old people. Happy now?"

Mandy sort of crumpled. She stared at me as though I'd stabbed her and then, after what seemed like forever, she shook her head and held out her hands to me.

"Billy I sorry, I not know. I not know," she said. "I not know. I am so very sorry."

It was a strange reaction, but she looked so upset I started to feel bad about shouting at her. "It's not your fault, Mandy," I said, before turning away from her and walking home.

I felt a bit shaken after the encounter with Mandy and went to sit with Gran, glad to be back in familiar surroundings.

I'd hardly had a chance to listen to Gran telling me about her day at The Colosseum in Rome, when Neelam appeared from the lift with a family, probably showing them round.

Behind Neelam was a man wearing a denim shirt with a long bit of oily hair plastered over his head. His tight, faded jeans made him look like he was permanently holding his breath, and they were tucked into brown cowboy boots. The woman was wearing a bright pink top over black leather trousers and boots with such high heels she had to cling onto the man's arm. Behind them was a boy.

It was Jude.

Instinctively, I moved behind Frank's chair to watch, but Frank, never one to understand subtlety, shouted, "Billy, what are you doing behind my chair?"

I swiftly moved behind the curtain to examine Mr Doyle. What a disappointment! Patrick Doyle, on his LinkedIn page, showed a man with a full head of brown hair, wearing a suit and tie. I couldn't see how this man talking to Neelam could possibly have let himself go that badly.

Jude was dragging behind his dad. "Dad just let me have my phone, I'm so bored," he moaned in a whiny, little-boy voice I'd never heard him use at school.

"Derek would ya just give 'im the thing," said the woman. "Shut 'im up for a few seconds."

Derek? My last hope was destroyed. All that work closing in on Jude, who I was sure had been keeping me away from the truth, and his dad had the wrong name.

I wasn't any closer to finding my parents, but I didn't have time to dwell on my disappointment because an interesting scene was unfolding in front of me.

"No Cindy," said Derek, swiping at Jude's head. "Did you hear what he said to me out there? He can't use words like that."

Jude's dad was just as bad as his mum, and I wondered if Cindy was his girlfriend. I looked around the room at the Oldies who were staring open-mouthed at the family. Beryl was working herself up to say something rude, I could tell. Pasqual was unhappily dancing his hands up and down, and Gran was bouncing Dardar's head on her lap.

"But Dad," wailed Jude. "Why did I have to come?

Jude's dad lifted his hand as if he was going to hit him, but Cindy caught his arm, swished her long hair and spoke through her teeth. "Derek, this ain't the time or place!"

"Ooh look at those fancy pants," Beryl suddenly burst out. "You'll enjoy living in this nuthouse!"

Neelam pretended she hadn't heard and quickly led Jude's dad and Cindy down one of the corridors.

Jude hung back, staring at Pascal who was now performing finger stretches and singing in French with his eyes shut.

"Nutter," said Jude, copying Pasqual's movements.

Beryl pointed a finger at him, "You're a strange looking boy. Why is your nose upside down?"

"You're all crazy in here!" said Jude, making his way over to Gran. I tensed, ready to knock him down if I had to.

Gran was squinting at Jude, trying to work out who he was. "Thank goodness you've come, doctor," she said. "My baby has this terrible rash, I think she's eaten too many strawberries. Would you mind taking a look?" She held out Dardar to Jude.

Jude seized the doll by the foot and held it upside down before running around the room with Dardar flying in big circles as Jude flapped his hands up and down. Luckily, Gran couldn't see what he was doing as her eyesight is so bad and she turned to Mary and said, "That's my husband you know, he's so good with children."

Gran might not be able to see, but I could, and I was about to confront Jude when Mary stood up. Mary appeared to be even more hunched over than usual and her lopsided face looked even more twisted. She slowly raised her head, and I was surprised to see she looked almost menacing.

On Jude's third circuit around the room he came face to face with Mary. He stopped abruptly and stared at Mary. I could clearly make out her angry words, "Who's that trip trapping over my bridge?"

Jude was terrified. A sharp gasp escaped from his mouth, and he dropped Dardar. Mary shuffled closer towards him. Jude turned and ran towards the lift. He desperately tried to press the buttons while turning his head to see Mary advancing on him. He frantically pulled and pushed the door, making whimpering noises. Mary had nearly reached the door and Jude looked like he was trying to press himself through it backwards. Mary went right up to him. It was too much for Jude. He opened his mouth and screamed a high-pitched howl. Mary walked straight past him and as she did, I heard her say quite clearly, "Georgie Porgie ran away."

Jude sank to the floor in a heap. I came out from behind the curtain and walked up to him. Jude looked at me with tears streaming down his face.

"Billy, what are you doing here?"

"I live here." The words jumped out of my mouth. What was I thinking of? I'd just told Jude I live in a care home.

"You *live* here?"

"Yes, I live here with these brilliant people. Frank over there is a war veteran, Pascal used to be a ballet dancer in Paris, and that's my Gran whose doll you nearly destroyed."

Mary came back from her little walk.

"Keep her away from me!" stuttered Jude. I took Mary's hand and she beamed at me.

"There came a big spider who sat down beside her and frightened Miss Muffet away!" she said.

"Mary," I grinned, "I think Jude has helped you get your voice back!"

As I helped Mary back to her chair, I saw Jude walk slowly over to where Dardar was lying. He picked up the doll and gave it gently back to Gran.

Neelam appeared with Derek and Cindy.

"Dad," said Jude who was standing next to Gran. "This might not be a bad place for Grandma."

His dad looked at him. "Shut it Jude," he said. "Nobody asked for your opinion."

"Yeah," said Cindy. "Why'd we care what *you* think?"

"I don't care what *any* of you think, but that man needs a makeover," said Beryl, pointing at Derek.

"Let's get outta here before we catch something," said Derek.

Neelam let them out through the coded door to take them downstairs, making me laugh with the look of pain she gave me before she turned back to the family. I thought about Jude. Perhaps having parents wasn't always a good thing. It explained a lot about Jude.

Twenty-Six

England, the present

Billy was becoming hard work.

Manya watched him loiter in the classroom before following Jude into the car park. What was he doing asking for more trouble with this boy? She felt like going straight up to him, grabbing him by the coat and telling him how she'd hurt her leg trying to protect him and could he just leave Jude alone. Then a car drove into the car park. It was the sort of car she might have seen in the centre of Moscow, but she certainly didn't expect to see anything so flamboyant in England.

Jude got into the car, which revved and swung round towards Billy. She flung herself in front of him without a second thought. She had to protect him at all costs. The car swerved away, out of school, and Billy started shouting at her. He was so ungrateful!

"Why did you do that?" he yelled, furiously.

"Why do you have to keep following him?" she demanded, sounding just as angry.

"If you must know, my parents disappeared eleven years ago when our house burnt down,"

Manya felt as though an electric current had passed through her. Every hair was standing on end, and she stared at him. Memories, hundreds of them, came flooding into her head.

"Billy, I sorry, I not know. I not know." She shook her head, and Billy ran off.

Manya ran to the park and found a bench overlooking the lake. The dusk and the still water helped to calm her, but her head was pounding. It hadn't been a dream at all, it was a memory.

She closed her eyes and let the scene unravel.

It must have been about eleven years ago. She had finished school and walked home by herself. Usually Babushka came to meet her, but today nobody had arrived. Manya had gone round to the back door which was open and had heard her father shouting.

"It's just for one night. Surely you can do this for me. She's your daughter too, although nobody would guess. I mean what have you ever done for her?"

"I'm going out," came her mother's voice.

"This is the most important night of my career, Inga, I can't take her with me," said Papa.

"Then leave her," came Mama's flat voice. "I'm going out."

"I can't leave her, she's six years old!"

Manya didn't know whether to run away or enter the kitchen.

“Papa?” she whispered. “Papa, where’s Babushka?”

Her father appeared at the door. “Manya, go and get some warm clothes. You have to come with me tonight. We’re going on a little trip.”

“Where’s Babushka?” Manya repeated.

“Babushka isn’t very well,” said her father. “She’s been taken to hospital for some tests.”

Manya cautiously entered the kitchen, but her mother was nowhere to be seen. She quickly went to her room, changed clothes, and when she came down, her father was waiting by the door.

“We need to leave,” he said. “Get in the car.”

After a short drive, they arrived at an aerodrome where Manya had to climb up steps to a small aeroplane. Her father came to sit next to her and gave her a plastic bottle with some orange liquid inside.

“Drink this,” he said.

“What is it?”

“Why do you always have to ask questions, Manya? Just drink it.”

The drink tasted bitter, and she struggled to swallow, but her father could get so angry, and he was already shouting at one of the other men in the plane.

“Galileo is mine!” he was shouting. “We agreed. Galileo is mine!”

Manya felt the plane begin to move forwards. She could hear the engines grow louder and the sudden pull of the jet’s thrust...

...and the next thing she remembered was waking up on the back seat of a car and seeing the flames. And the screaming woman. She was shouting for her child. Two men dragged her towards a van and bundled her into the back.

Then three more men appeared and climbed into a second van.

Where was Papa? She got out of the car and looked around, but all she could see were other houses with lights coming on and people running towards the house. She backed away, nearly tripping on the kerb. The sound of a siren was coming closer, and Manya sat down at the edge of the road, hugging her knees, rocking backwards and forwards.

Firefighters arrived. Two were already breaking down the front door, shouting words she couldn't understand.

The firefighters carried two people out of the blazing building. First an old lady and then a small boy.

As the firefighter gently passed the child over, the little boy turned his head. It seemed to Manya that he was looking straight at her, and she shivered involuntarily, despite the heat from the fire.

Suddenly, it was as though the whole world had exploded. A huge ball of flames leapt upwards from the house. A figure was running towards her, towards the car. He flung open the back door and pulled her arm.

"Get in, Manya! Get in right now!"

"'Scuse me love," said a voice. "Are you 'ere for the night?"

Manya opened her eyes to see an old woman wearing at least three layers of clothing and holding four plastic bags stuffed full of more clothes.

"Net, I mean no," she replied. For a moment she had thought she was on the bench in Lopatinsky Park. She stood up, making way for the woman, who started arranging her belongings on the bench.

Wandering back to Autumn Days she thought about the little boy. It was Billy. She had been there when Billy's house had burnt down, and she had watched his parents being taken away in two separate vans. And she remembered who had told her to get in the car: it was Papa.

The same purple and gold Rolls Royce from the school car park was pulling away as she arrived back at Autumn Days, but Manya didn't give it a second thought. She was trying to piece together how her father could have been involved with Billy and his parents. Had he been in on the whole thing from the beginning? Had Goar V and Tatiana been part of his plans? Had her father deceived his own daughter in an elaborate plan to use her for his own devices? No, no, no!

She sat at her desk looking at three photos in front of her. The first was Babushka, sitting in her rocking chair smiling and wearing the emerald ring she had given to Manya.

The second photo was of Manya's parents. She didn't want to look at her mother's cold expression, so she covered the face with her finger and looked at her father. What was he up to and how was he involved with everything that had happened?

The third photo was of Billy in his school uniform and Manya thought back to the day he had given it to her.

"Mandy I'm not sure if you want this, but school gave me loads and Neelam said you might like it," he'd said. "I made the frame myself, out of an old cereal box."

Manya had been so surprised and touched, she had burst into tears.

"I knew you wouldn't like it!" said Billy.

"I love so much this gift! I very happy you think to give me so beautiful present. I put it next Babushka, she most important person in life for me."

"Not your parents?" asked Billy.

Manya shook her head.

"Bit like me then," he'd said simply, and went back to sit with Gran.

"Neelam, I sorry," she said, two hours later. "I must return with father for talking to him. It very much important."

"Oh dear," said Neelam. "I'm sorry to hear that. Is there anything I can do to help? When are you leaving?"

"Now," replied Manya. "Taxi waits downstairs. I hope I am being back in some days. So sorry."

How could she explain everything to Neelam? Or to Billy? She would confront her father, discover the truth, and return to England once she had found Billy's parents.

Twenty-Seven

England, the present

I felt a bit down the next day when I told Katie what had happened and how I'd found out Jude's dad wasn't Patrick Doyle.

"I really thought we were on to something," I said.

"Don't worry," said Katie. "Something else will turn up. I'm not going to stop looking for clues."

At school, Jude behaved as if he'd never been to Autumn Days, except he seemed self-conscious when I was nearby. I didn't have time for him and his stupid gang. There were more important things to think about.

When I got home I did my usual thing of talking to Gran first, and that was when I noticed Mary's chair was empty.

"Where's Mary?" I asked Gran.

"Yes, I looked in all the shops, but I couldn't find any curtains that matched," she replied, which didn't exactly answer my question. I sometimes wonder what Gran talked about before she had dementia.

Neelam came over. "I'm afraid Mary isn't at all well. The doctor thinks she might have had another stroke and needs to stay in bed. I'm going to keep a close eye on her."

"Can I go and see her?" I asked. "I don't understand. She was in such good form yesterday, and even speaking properly. What happened?"

"I wish I knew why these things happen. One day people can seem fine, even a bit better, and the next they become really poorly. But go and see her, she would love to see you."

I went into Mary's room. She was lying in bed with her beads in her hands, running them through her fingers. I went up close and said, "Hello Mary, what happened? You were brilliant yesterday with Jude."

Mary opened her eyes and smiled at me.

She reached out her hand and took mine, squeezing it gently just like she always did, but this time there was a slight shake of her head. It was as if she'd had enough of being old, of not being able to say what she wanted to say, of everything being a struggle.

Then she pressed her beads into my hands and tried to say something, but it sounded like, "Frong."

I tried to work out what she was saying. "Your beads, I know they're special, why are you giving them to me?"

Mary took a deep breath and her face showed how much she was concentrating. "Gi da Frong," she said.

I felt helpless and repeated the words aloud. Suddenly they made more sense. "Give to Frong, to Frank?" I asked.

Mary looked relieved and nodded, letting the beads fall into my hand. I looked at her misty eyes and had the strange sensation they were telling me something. It was as though Mary was trying to say goodbye to me.

I waited until she'd fallen asleep, before creeping towards the door. I looked back one last time and suddenly felt really sad. I walked slowly back to my room, sat on my bed and said a prayer. I prayed for Mary, for Gran and for all the old people who have to get dementia.

The next morning I lay in bed looking at Mary's beads on the desk feeling empty. I hadn't given them to Frank yet and wondered why she wanted him to have them. They were just a long string of round beads with a random pattern and a big silver clasp. I hoped Mary might be feeling better this morning and went to find Neelam.

Neelam's little flat is opposite my room. The door was open, and I could see through to her sitting room. She was standing with her back towards me, looking out through the window. I knocked quietly and she turned around. Her face was sad.

"What's happened?" I asked.

"It's...oh Billy...I'm so sorry but Mary's gone."

"Gone where?" I asked, not wanting to hear the answer.

"I sat with her until really late last night and she didn't seem very well, so I called the doctor," said Neelam. "An ambulance came, but by the time it arrived Mary had died. She fell asleep and just stopped breathing. She was very peaceful."

I couldn't speak. Mary *had* been saying goodbye. Neelam and I sat on her sofa together and I felt numb. Other people had died at Autumn Days, after all, most of them are very old, but never one of my special friends.

Neelam and I sat together for a long time.

When people die at Autumn Days, their photo is put in a frame and taken down to the reception area. I didn't like it because sometimes, when I came back from school, there'd be a new photo. When Gran was ill, I was scared I'd come home and see her photo in a frame. Now that Mary had died, I sort of understood the point of it. It's a sign that the person won't be forgotten. I asked Neelam if I could choose the picture.

"I want to find one where she's wearing her red dress. Do you remember when she used to walk around with her clipboard?"

We both laughed. I was so sad Mary had died, but it felt good to talk about her and to think about the funny things she'd done, and the good times we'd had.

Neelam said I could miss school and I was glad because I wouldn't have been able to concentrate. I went to get Mary's beads and took them to Frank who was wiping his eyes with a huge white handkerchief.

"She was an absolute corker, that Mary," said Frank. "One of the bravest ladies you could ever 'ope to meet."

"She was brave?" I asked. "Did you know Mary before she came to live here?"

Frank looked at me as though I was completely stupid. Then he looked confused and glanced around before lowering his voice. "Of course I knew Mary, she worked at Bletchley, you know. None of us would be 'ere at all if it weren't for Mary."

"She asked me to give these to you," I said, handing him the beads.

"Well done, lad," said Frank. "You've done a very important thing there, and one day I'll be able to explain," he looked around suspiciously. "But not just now."

I didn't have a clue what he was talking about; he'd probably been watching too many spy films.

A message came through on my phone from Katie and I went to my room. I'd contacted her earlier to tell her about Mary, and she'd messaged back saying she was sad too because she really liked Mary. But this was about something else:

I've found something.

Twenty-Eight

Moscow, the present

Landing in Moscow, Manya remembered back to how it used to be when Babushka had taken her to see Red Square, so many years ago. Things had changed since then.

The kiosks, the little stalls selling newspapers, sweets and groceries, they'd nearly all gone. Babushka had bought her a bag filled with honey-covered chak-chaks and her fingers had become all sticky. Now, all she could see were burger bars and coffee houses cramming themselves into the spaces between jewellery shops and fashion boutiques.

She remembered how they had travelled in a rickety old brown carriage from Smolensk. The new train she was taking home was silver, sleek and fast. Too fast. What was she going to say to her father?

She took a taxi for the final part of her journey and asked the driver to drop her at a short distance from the house to give her a few extra minutes.

Standing on the doorstep, Manya wished she'd tried to make herself look more presentable. Her hair was unbrushed and she hadn't slept properly. She took a deep breath and rang the doorbell. There was no sound of movement inside the house, just the distant strains of Handel's Water Music. She rang again. And again. At last, slow, heavy footsteps could be heard approaching the door. Was Papa ill?

The door opened slowly, but it wasn't her father. It was Mrs Molchalin.

Manya didn't know how to address this stranger who had never acknowledged her existence.

"Where is Papa?"

Mrs Molchalin's eyes looked straight past Manya as if she couldn't see her own dishevelled daughter on the doorstep.

"Mr Molchalin died three weeks ago," she said, shutting the door again.

Manya felt her world come crashing in on her. How could this be? How had he died? She stared blankly at the door, before turning around and walking slowly away from her childhood home for the last time.

She thought back to the time when Papa had been so proud of her. How he'd always been so ambitious for her and so excited to think that one day she might attend the great Moscow State University. "Manya, one day you will make the name Molchalin great," he always said.

What if he'd been trying to contact her to tell her he was unwell and he couldn't find her? She should have ignored Tatiana and told him she was in England.

What about the nightmares, the fire and her father's involvement in the kidnapping of Billy's parents. He wouldn't be able to tell her what it was all about. It just didn't make sense.

She decided to go back to Moscow and find Feliks at school. It was still term-time, and although he must have thought she'd disappeared off the face of the earth, he might be pleased to see her.

As the bus pulled up outside Kolmogorov, she began to feel nervous. Feliks had always been a good and reliable friend to her, but she had never done anything except get him involved in trouble of some sort or another. Why would he be pleased to see her? It was getting dark, and she knew the students would be having dinner. She crossed the quad and peered in through the dining-room windows. Everyone looked carefree, young and happy. That could have been her if she'd listened to Feliks, instead of following her own stupid quest for adventure.

There was Feliks. He was sitting with a group of students who were laughing. He looked happy, he looked relaxed, and he was sitting next to Karine. Manya stepped away from the window stifling a sob. There was no way Feliks would want to help her again. He was with Karine, and the time had come for Manya to leave him alone. She ran back to the bus stop, where a bus was about to depart. She didn't care where it was going, she just had to get away from school. The bus's destination showed above the driver's head: *Novotel Moscow Kievskaya.* That would do for tonight. She'd spend the night in a hotel, and maybe her head would be clearer in the morning.

After a sleepless night in the hotel room, with air-conditioning scratching her throat, Manya dragged herself out of bed. She went to the window. The streets below were grey, the buildings were grey and even the sky had grey clouds scudding across it. The scene matched her mood. She had tossed and turned in the night, mourning the unexpected loss of her father, and the realisation that she had lost Feliks, her only friend. There was only one thing she wanted to do now. She reached into the big pocket of her overcoat and pulled out the photo Billy had given her.

"Don't worry Billy," she said, "I'm going to find your parents."

There was a knock at the door.

Who could it be?

She checked her phone. It was off. But it had been on when she arrived in Russia and when she had gone to find Feliks. With a sinking feeling she shuffled slowly across the room. Surely Tatiana hadn't traced her movements all the way from England to Moscow? Would she be standing on the other side of the door now, ready to rebuke Manya for leaving her post? Couldn't she just leave her alone?

She put her hand out and slowly, cautiously opened the door.

Her eyes widened in shock, her legs buckled, and she sank to the floor.

Twenty-Nine

England, the present

Katie was hopping from one foot to the other, looking as if she was about to burst.

"What is it?" I asked. "What've you found?"

We still had five minutes before school started, and she led me away from the main entrance.

"I've been doing a bit more digging, and I think I might have found something!"

"About my parents?"

"Yes. I've been searching for information about missing people. It's almost impossible to find stuff because most of it's confidential. But then I found this short paragraph from a local newspaper in Yorkshire. I took a screenshot."

She held out her phone for me to read, but I didn't think it would be very useful because I didn't know anyone in Yorkshire.

Local Scientist Disappears, said the headline. *Reports are emerging from the UK Space Agency (UKSA) concerning the disappearance of an eminent scientist. According to local sources, the scientist, who has not been named, had been living in the village of Tapfield, North Yorkshire. Mr Smythe, a neighbour, revealed to the North Yorkshire Times that the family moved out of the village very suddenly with no mention of a forwarding address. Local police have declined to comment, but the UKSA have admitted that investigations are underway.*

That was about all it said, and I was disappointed. "Is that it?"

"Have you seen the date?" asked Katie.

I scrolled up. The date was two days after the fire.

"So you think my dad might be the missing scientist?" I asked.

"Not exactly," said Katie. "The missing scientist was a woman."

We spent a whole weekend searching for more information about the missing scientist. During our investigation we found an interesting report on a missing spacecraft which had been located on Mars, and another article which mentioned a missing scientist, but the date was 1961 and I didn't think my mum would have even been born.

I was back to where I started, and the only thing that lifted my bad mood was our upcoming football match. It was the most important match of the year, the local Derby: Evergreen Grove versus Copper Street College. We were determined to win this year, having lost for the past four years.

When I got home there weren't any decent cakes for tea because Gordon didn't like making them and Mandy had gone back to Russia to see her dad. Neelam told me she'd gone, and I hoped it wasn't because of what I'd said the other day in the school car park. She was so weird when I told her about the fire, apologising as if it was her fault. I decided to be nicer to her when she got back.

Katie and I were both in the football team, and so was Jude. I hoped he might be more friendly after his visit to Autumn Days, maybe even pass me the ball sometimes. I reckoned he was embarrassed about me seeing his dad's car too. If I ever had a lot of money, a purple and gold Rolls Royce would be the last thing I'd buy.

We had football practices after school on Tuesday, Wednesday and Thursday. Mr Castle was so intense about the big match, I didn't really have time to think about the disastrous investigation, the search for my parents, or about Mary.

On Thursday evening I set up one of the corridors for skills practice. I had to take down a couple of pictures, a mirror and a long feathery thing. Pascal lent me his zimmer frame as a goal.

I walked onto the 'pitch' with Dardar as my mascot, waving to the capacity crowd. The stands were filling rapidly and even Beryl was asking for her wheelchair to be moved closer to the action. Beryl's so nosey she probably didn't want to miss whatever was going on, or an opportunity to make a rude remark.

"What's going on here?" she demanded.

"Welcome to Wembley, Beryl," I said. "You are about to witness the skills, the strength and the stamina of one of the best English footballers who has ever lived."

"So where is he?" she asked.

"It's me! You're going to watch me play football down the corridor."

"I'd rather eat my hearing aids," she said, and wheeled herself back to the TV.

On Friday, the day of the match, the players were allowed to leave their last lesson fifteen minutes early to get changed and have a final quick practice. Mr Castle was red in the face, his forehead all scrunched up and his legs all jittery. He was much more nervous than we were.

"Right lads," he said, spitting the words out. "Remember the work we've done this week. Keep the defence tight and don't let them near the goal. Forwards, once you've got the ball, sprint up and make sure to pass before you're tackled. Now get going and play your socks off!"

He was making us all feel nervous. I got into position and jogged up and down to keep warm. Slobbery Big Ben and Tyrone were on the side lines. Tyrone was wearing shades and had his hands in his pockets, trying to look cool. Big Ben had volunteered to look after the end-of-match doughnuts. It was a massive bag, and he was drooling like a dog.

I looked over to the car park where some supporters were arriving, and blinked to check I wasn't dreaming. A big minibus had arrived. Neelam and Gordon were unloading three wheelchairs.

The whistle started the game and Jude kicked the ball back to Katie. I hoped she wouldn't pass it to me as I was distracted by Beryl shouting from the side-line.

"Aw, is it football? I thought it was going to be cricket."

Katie passed the ball, and I messed up by giving it straight to the oppo.

"Crikey, it's worse than I thought!" shouted Beryl.

Frank was more encouraging, "Come on Billy! Come on green ones!" he was yelling. He was wearing a Spurs hat and scarf. *My* Spurs hat and scarf!

The first half was a disaster. When the whistle blew for half time, we were 3-0 down. Dylan had done some great saves, but Mr Castle was furious. "What are you doing?" he shouted at us. "This isn't what we practised. Get back on that pitch and start playing football!"

It wasn't exactly a motivational speech and we all felt pretty useless as we took our positions. The other team were still sitting in their goal mouth eating oranges.

Beryl started singing *Happy Birthday* at the top of her voice.

I looked at our team. We were all strolling back onto the pitch with hunched shoulders as the opposition sprinted back to their positions.

"Come on green ones! Let's beat them bloomin' Jerries. We can do this," shouted Frank.

Their centre forward kicked the ball back to one of his team's midfielders and out of nowhere Jude raced forwards, intercepted the ball and dribbled it up the pitch. Then a quick pass to Katie who put it in the back of the net!

There was a loud whoop from the side-lines, and even Beryl was clapping.

Suddenly my team looked confident. So confident, we scored two more goals in fifteen minutes, one from Jude and one from Sid. 3-3.

Five minutes to go and I heard a new voice from the side of the pitch.

"Come on Billy mate, make it one more for me!" It was Louis.

I hadn't had a great game and I was disappointed not to have put on a good show for my supporters. But there they were, that strange family of mine cheering me on. I had a lot of complicated things in my life, but at that moment, everything was good, and I felt a surge of energy. My legs were light, and I sprinted forwards to get into position. Katie and Jude did a quick little one two to get past the defence and then I was there. A short pass from Jude...

...everything went into slow motion, "Put it in Billy!" The ball was too far to the right, I wasn't going to reach it. I took back my right foot, practically did the splits in mid-air and bam! Smack into the back of the net as the final whistle blew!

Trying to ignore the pain in my groin, I joined in the celebrations before lining up to shake hands with the other team who were furious at losing in the last few seconds. Then one of them started laughing and pointing at the car park. The purple and gold Rolls Royce had just pulled in. "Doyle's Cleaning Co.' gleaming on the side.

Jude was trying to hide behind Sid, but Big Ben shouted, "Hey Jude, yer old man's here. Bit late."

One of the opposition whistled. What does he do, your dad? That Roller must've cost a bomb!"

"Nah," said Jude. "My dad's a total waster. He didn't earn his money, he won it on the lottery."

Thirty

Moscow, the present

"Papa?" gasped Manya looking up from the floor in shock.

"Manya, it's good to see you."

Mr Molchalin helped his daughter to her feet and led her to a chair inside the hotel room. He went to the door to check it had closed firmly before sitting opposite her.

"Mama told me you were dead," whispered Manya, barely able to speak.

"You know as well as I do, your mother has never been a reliable source of information."

"What's wrong with her?" asked Manya.

"I tried to persuade her to get help, and she refused. I made appointments with doctors, but she wouldn't go."

"So you left her?" asked Manya.

"I tried to be patient," said Mr Molchalin. "She became more and more difficult to live with. She became aggressive towards me, and I was left with no choice. I had to move out, and for her, that meant I was dead."

"How did you know I was here?"

"It's a long story, but Manya, I'm so happy to see you, I was so worried."

"I've been in England. I've been working for a secret organisation. I'm going to make the name Molchalin great, Papa!"

"I know, Manya, I'm proud of what you've achieved, and now you're ready."

"Ready for what?"

"To join me of course," he said, as though it was obvious. "To work with me, and the timing couldn't be better. Your ability to dig into computer systems is going to help me resolve an awkward and unpleasant situation."

"What situation?"

"That's what you came back for isn't it?" said her father.

"No!" cried Manya. "I haven't come here to join you. I've come for answers. I've come for Billy's parents."

It was as though her father hadn't heard. "I want you to come with me," he said. "I've got something to show you. Pack your bag and meet me in the lobby. I've paid the bill."

And with that he was gone.

In a haze of bewilderment, Manya did as she was told. She packed her bag, took the lift to the ground floor, and followed her father out of the hotel, where a large black Mercedes was waiting. The driver leapt out of the car and opened the rear door for Manya. She slipped onto the cream leather seat next to her father.

"Whose car is this?" she asked.

"It's mine," said Mr Molchalin. "I've been waiting for this day for a very long time. Probably your whole life, and now you must give me the pleasure of enjoying it."

Manya tried to collect her thoughts. How did Papa know she'd been in England? She sat in silence as the car purred softly, skirting the banks of the wide Moskva River and on towards the Presnensky District, where the buildings became taller and altogether more impressive.

Finally, they drew up outside a tall, glass-fronted building and Manya looked out of the window to see the words, 'DM Engineering' engraved into the glass above the entrance.

A man wearing a black suit and dark glasses stepped up to open the door for Mr Molchalin, while the driver opened Manya's door.

She followed her father through the swing doors, into the building where a receptionist wearing a red jacket nodded politely and said, "Good morning, Mr Molchalin."

They walked straight through the grand entrance to a lobby with four lifts on either side. A man wearing the same red jacket as the receptionist, was holding the lift, and he stood back to let Manya and her father in.

"Papa, what is this place?" asked Manya.

"All in good time," said Mr Molchalin, mysteriously.

From the lift, Manya could see across Moscow. Higher and higher to the forty-second floor. The view was breathtaking. Manya found herself being ushered out of the lift and into a large office with an enormous desk.

Mr Molchalin stepped back into the corridor for a moment to speak to a tall thin woman with a very serious face.

"Zoran is waiting," she said.

"Just give me a couple of minutes," said Mr Molchalin, grimly.

He entered his office, walked around the desk and sat in the black leather chair behind it. He motioned for Manya to sit opposite.

"I don't understand what this is all about," said Manya. "Why are we here and why do you have this huge office?"

Mr Molchalin smiled at his daughter.

"I have become rather important," he said, smugly. "This company is called Dimitri Molchalin Engineering. I have always been an ambitious man and I wanted you to be ambitious too. You always showed so much promise at school, and now you're ready to join me. Maybe you'll take over the company one day." He paused for a moment, and Manya opened her mouth to say something, but her father was already talking into a speaker on his desk. "You can come in now," he said.

There was a quick tap on the door, and Manya looked round as someone stepped into the room.

"Tatiana!"

"It's good to see you, Manya," she said.

Thirty-One

England, the present

It took a long time for the Oldies to get back to Autumn Days. I'd gone ahead with Louis, and we'd practically demolished a whole packet of chocolate digestives by the time the others got back.

As Neelam pushed Gran's wheelchair into the lounge, the news came on the TV. I looked up and saw a building on fire and nudged Louis who always likes a good fire story.

"*... after an apparent tip-off, police finally tracked him down to a disused schoolhouse on an uninhabited island in the Outer Hebrides. As the gang escaped, a massive explosion destroyed the building and fire-fighting helicopters were deployed to extinguish the fire. Further investigation has revealed three gas canisters as the cause of the explosion.*"

I looked at the fire blazing on the island. Three gas canisters! I looked at Louis and Neelam, and I could tell they were thinking the same as me.

"Three gas canisters!" I said, aloud. "Is that normal, or could there be a connection? Could it be the same people who destroyed my house?"

"I wouldn't have thought so," said Louis, looking like he *did* think so. "Let's just keep an eye on the news."

It was hard to sleep that night. I had a nightmare about Mr Castle bringing gas canisters to school so he could blow up the gym. Louis came in his fire engine, and Gran was driving. Jude appeared and told me we had to score a goal or the whole school would burn down. It sounds funny now, but I woke up with my heart beating so loudly I thought I could hear footsteps, which was even more scary.

It was Saturday, so I didn't have to go to school. I went to sit with Gran who was looking at a newspaper which was the right way up for a change. I thought she might actually be reading it, she seemed to be concentrating so hard. Suddenly she started shouting, "Immerson! Immerson!" She was very upset, waving the paper around, "Immerson!"

Neelam rushed over and tried to extract the paper, but Gran wouldn't let go. She was crying and shouting, and we couldn't understand what she was saying. I looked at the newspaper. The page she'd been looking at had the headline "*Scottish base for Russian missile?*" and two pictures. One was of the fire and the other was the photo of a group of men running. I'm pretty sure Gran couldn't read the small writing under the pictures, but I read it. Under one picture it said, *Abandoned schoolhouse ablaze.*

And under the other it said, *Russian gang fleeing the burning building.*

Was Gran remembering the fire? Might she be able to remember anything else?

"Gran are you alright?" I asked. She was gripping onto the newspaper with one hand and pointing at the photos with the other. Then she let it drop to the floor and put her head in her hands. "Immerson," she muttered as if she was in despair.

Neelam called the doctor.

I didn't want to upset Gran, although if the fire in the paper reminded her of our fire, I needed to seize the moment before she forgot again. Neelam said I shouldn't mention the fire as it might unsettle her; she'd only just recovered from the last illness when she had to go to hospital, and she needed to be kept calm. I'd already lost Mary and I didn't want to lose Gran too.

I picked up the newspaper and tried to read the article. It was difficult to figure it out. The police had been searching for some Russian who they thought might be making a missile, and they'd located suspicious activity on the island. The police arrived too late, and the gang had flown off in a helicopter, leaving the burning building. Undercover detectives posing as fishermen had taken the photo of the gang running away.

A close-up photo of Zoran Krasnov showed a man with a beard and dark hair. When Neelam wasn't looking, I put the photo in front of Gran, but she didn't react. Yet another lead resulting in a dead end.

Katie came round on Sunday, although she couldn't stay long as she had an ultimate frisbee match. I showed her the image of the men running to the helicopter and she examined it closely.

"It's no good, I can't see what the connection could be," said Katie. "Why would Gran get so upset about this photo? Is it something to do with the helicopter, do you think? When she says Immerson does she point to anything in particular?"

"I'm pretty sure she's pointing at one of the men," I said.

We spent the next hour looking up people called Immerson. It wasn't easy. There were plenty of people with the name Emmerson, but I was certain Gran was saying Im, not Em.

In the end we only found three people in the whole world with the surname Immerson: Bill, Lori and Marvin, who all lived in America.

Katie had to leave, but I asked Neelam if I could keep the TV on the news channel to keep up to date with the Scottish story.

I tried to get Gran to do some mindfulness colouring. Some of the Oldies like colouring; Gran isn't one of them. I couldn't get her to hold the pencils, so I started colouring the picture myself. Suddenly Gran started banging the arms of her chair.

"Babberchook Immerson! Immerson!" she shouted. I looked at the TV. It was the same photo of the men on the island running away from the fire.

"Gran," I said. "Do you know one of those men? Is his name Mr Immerson?"

Gran shook her head violently, "Immerson! Im..mer...son!" she cried, pointing at the screen.

"I don't know Immerson," I said, trying to stay calm while Gran kept banging her chair. The picture had gone, and Neelam came rushing over. I stood up and went nearer the TV to try to hear what was being said, but it was difficult with Gran shouting. Beryl joined in because Beryl loves shouting.

"Why are you all shouting?" she shouted, "It's so noisy!"

It was too late. The news had moved to the next story and Neelam turned off the TV.

Gran knew one of those men, who could he be? I found a Sunday newspaper, but the name Immerson didn't appear anywhere. It was all about Zoran Krasnov.

Neelam was trying to calm Gran down with a cup of tea, and Gran was still saying the name 'Immerson' over and over and looking around the room as if she hoped somebody else might understand.

I went back to the newspaper.

"Foreign Secretary, Simon Riven has confirmed the wanted Russian arms dealer, Zoran Krasnov is believed to have escaped by helicopter from a Scottish island with four other members of his team. 'We will leave no stone unturned,' said Mr Riven last night. 'If any members of this highly dangerous gang are still in the UK, we will find them,' he added."

There was the same photo of the running men. The photo that made Gran upset. I took the paper to Neelam. Gran was half asleep, so I spoke quietly.

"Gran knows one of the men in the photo," I whispered. "She keeps calling one of them Immerson. Can I show her when she wakes up?"

"We can't risk upsetting her." Neelam whispered back, "She's too frail, and you saw how distressed she became when she saw that picture yesterday."

"What if it's something to do with my parents?"

"If it has anything to do with your parents, I'm sure the police will be in touch."

If this was the breakthrough I'd been hoping for, I wasn't going to hang around waiting for the police. I needed to take action.

Thirty-Two

Moscow, the present

Manya looked from Tatiana to her father and back to Tatiana,

"You work together?" she whispered.

"Close," said her father. "Tatiana works for me. She was the person who enabled your incredible learning experience."

"Manya, didn't you ever wonder how I knew all about you?" asked Tatiana.

"You said you could use my skills," Manya said, bitterly.

"We *did* use your skills. We still need your skills," continued Tatiana. "However, your father has rather a lot of meetings today." She looked at Mr Molchalin and nodded her head. "I can take it from here," she said.

"Excuse me, Manya," said her father. "I have to go to this meeting, but stay in here and I'll join you as soon as I can."

He left the room. Tatiana immediately went to sit in Mr Molchalin's chair and folded her arms. Her friendly expression disappeared.

"What are you doing back here?" she demanded. "Your mission isn't complete."

"I've come back for Billy's parents," said Manya, boldly. "Why didn't you tell me the truth?"

Tatiana leaned back and let out a shrill laugh. "The truth? Do you, of all people, think you deserve the truth?"

Manya was taken aback. Tatiana had hit a nerve because she was right. Throughout her life, Manya had never hesitated to lie and cheat. At least that was how she used to be. Since living in England with Billy and the Oldies she had changed.

"But, since you're here, you might as well hear how clever your Papa has been," said Tatiana. "He had it all planned from the beginning. He employed me before you even started at Kolmogorov. It was his idea to create the fake team called Goar V. Don't look so surprised, the messages you intercepted were all from me using multiple phones to make it look like I was the leader of an all-female group. You should be proud of your father. He has masterminded an organisation in which you are a tiny cog. Yet he always wanted you to be part of it."

"Why did I have to go through all that training?" asked Manya.

"Your father insisted that you should be able to defend yourself. You have no idea of the danger surrounding your mission."

"Danger?" scoffed Manya. "Taking photos of a thirteen-year-old and discouraging a little pack of bullies? I can't see the danger."

"Sending photos is essential," said Tatiana. "Galileo won't continue to work for us without them."

"What do you mean? Who is Galileo?"

"Galileo is Billy's mum," said Tatiana.

"You've been using the photos to blackmail her!" exclaimed Manya, aghast at the realisation. "Do you mean you've been showing her my photos of Billy to force her to work for you?"

"For your father," said Tatiana. "She's a brilliant scientist. Many years ago, in England, she was working on a British telescope so powerful it would be able to see into a black hole. This had never been done before, and we couldn't let the British beat us to it. Galileo came to work with us eleven years ago and brought the knowledge of the telescope with her."

"You kidnapped her!" said Manya. "You kidnapped Billy's mum for a telescope?" She was near tears.

"Not me, it was your father," said Tatiana.

Manya couldn't believe what she was hearing.

"And you will be pleased to hear that the telescope has helped him to build his empire," continued Tatiana. "He even named it Mantel: Manya's Telescope. Doesn't that make you feel proud?"

"No, it disgusts me," said Manya. "I am ashamed to have been part of all this. He must send Billy's mum home now."

"We are all proud to have been part of such an important project," said Tatiana, ignoring Manya's reaction.

Another thought struck Manya. "Where's Billy's dad?"

"We don't have access to him. He was not part of the deal," said Tatiana.

"The deal?"

Tatiana faltered, as though she had said too much. She stood up and left Manya in her father's imposing office looking out over the top of Moscow.

Manya went into the bathroom and splashed water over her face. Looking at herself in the mirror, she saw anger in her eyes. How could her father have deceived her like this? He had used her, made her an unwitting accomplice in a scheme he would probably classify as 'helping the Motherland'.

As she walked back to her father's office, Tatiana appeared again. Manya thought quickly and decided she needed to take a very risky opportunity. She'd seen Tatiana in the gym enough times to know the woman was strong, fit and agile. Manya made sure her balance was poised, glanced over her shoulder to gauge Tatiana's exact position and, without a sound, she whisked her right foot, timing her kick perfectly. Tatiana was on the floor, looking up at Manya with a shocked and dazed expression. She was up again immediately, wary and poised to attack back.

"Izolda taught me well," said Manya, ready for the counter-attack, but Tatiana's gym sessions hadn't prepared her for judo kicks, and Manya, took her down again with an illegal Kani Basami, grasping Tatiana's head in a tight leg lock.

"One slight twist of my knee is going to break your neck," said Manya, not entirely sure if this was correct, but it was the best she could come up with in the heat of the moment.

Tatiana stopped struggling and Manya took her chance. "Where is Galileo?" she asked, squeezing her knees tighter around Tatiana's neck.

"I don't know," rasped Tatiana, struggling to breathe.

"Tell me now!" shouted Manya.

"Your father sent her to The Block. Loosen your grip Manya!"

"What is The Block? I'm not letting you go until you tell me, and it had better be the truth."

"Behind the veterinary centre in the Chertanovo district," spluttered Tatiana.

Leaving Tatiana sprawling on the floor, Manya dashed back to her father's polished office, straight to the middle drawer of his desk. As she expected, his keys were hidden inside an old bag of sweets, a trick she had watched many times as a child. Grabbing the car key, the key card, and her small bag of belongings, she dashed to the lift and opened it using the card, knowing Tatiana would have raised the alarm by now.

Mr Molchalin's private lift descended swiftly to the ground floor and Manya ran past the front desk, relieved that the receptionist barely glanced up. Through the revolving doors, the man in the dark glasses was talking to her father's driver, a little way from the black Mercedes. She slowed to a walk and raised her hand as casually as she could.

"Papa has lent me the car for a couple of hours," she said.

"I can take you," said the driver, reaching into his pocket for his own set of car keys, but Manya was already in the driver's seat. The car was much bigger than the grey Lada, but the break and pedals were in the same place and, as Manya revved the car, she smiled to herself. "Thanks for the driving lessons, Papa," she said, pulling away from DM Engineering.

After driving for about ten minutes, Manya found herself in the centre of Moscow and pulled over to set the navigation to the veterinary centre in the Chertanovo district. The estimated journey was half an hour. It would give her time to decide what to say to Billy's mum when she found her.

She began to enjoy driving the shiny black Mercedes and was surprised how much respect other drivers gave her, compared with the impatience she was used to in the old Lada, but she felt jittery, especially when a couple of police cars sped past with flashing lights.

Directions on her phone led Manya straight to the run-down district of Chertanovo, and she had no trouble locating the veterinary centre. She stopped the car and got out. A group of men, sitting on the ground with their legs stretched out, turned to stare at her. Locking the car, she walked around the large building, expecting to find another smart office bearing the sign DM Engineering.

A small, cream-coloured building sat desolately in front of her, covered with badly drawn graffiti. Was this The Block? Some of the windows had been shattered, and green netting had been roughly attached to the crumbling walls as a meagre attempt to stop anyone entering. Had Galileo been sent here? She carefully picked her way across the rubble towards the entrance and pushed the door. It creaked open, revealing a bleak hallway, empty apart from a few plastic bags strewn here and there.

It was silent in the building and, as Manya explored the rooms, she began to feel uneasy. If Galileo had been brought here, surely she would have escaped. Unless, of course, she was locked inside a room.

A dusty red carpet covered the staircase leading up to the second floor, and Manya was grateful for the sunlight streaming in through the filthy windows. She wouldn't have been brave enough to go further in the dark.

"Hello," Manya called quietly in English. "Is somebody here?"

There was no response, so she started looking through the upstairs rooms. A brown jacket lay in the corner of one room, and cigarette stubs littered the floor. Back on the landing she noticed a dark, windowless corridor, leading away from the stairs with a closed door at the end.

"I look for Billy's mum," she called again, her voice sounding shrill and tense as she approached the door. Placing her fingers lightly on the knob, she twisted. It was locked. She tried again, pushing harder, and this time she heard something behind the door. Something was moving. Manya's anxiety was increasing by the second. What if Billy's mum had been locked in the room and was too hurt to call out. Maybe she was gagged, or worse, unconscious.

There was nothing else for it, she had to get into the room. Time to use her Taekwondo again; a quick front kick should do it.

Another sound from behind the door strengthened her resolve. She took one step back, raised her right leg and kicked the door with all her strength. The catch gave way and the door swung open.

A flurry of grey wings brushed her head, and Manya recoiled in disgust at the scene in front of her. At least seven dead pigeons lay on the floor. A jagged gap in the window had allowed the birds in, but they hadn't been able to find their way out. Just one had survived and had already found an exit. Manya saw it flying away, back to freedom. There was nothing else in the room.

She'd been tricked. She felt the vibration of her phone in her pocket as a message came through.

Big mistake

It was from Tatiana.

Yes, Tatiana, you have made a very big mistake, thought Manya, turning off her phone.

How could I have been so stupid? she asked herself angrily as she returned to the car. *Why did I believe her?*

The men who had been sitting on the ground were examining the car, probably debating whether it was worth breaking into. They leered at Manya as she approached, however she was so angry there was no room for fear.

"Stand back from that car right now!" she shouted, the venom in her voice enough to make them jump back.

Surprised at her own audacity, she got in the car and sped off in the direction of the airport. There was only one place she wanted to be right now, and it wasn't Russia. She had failed to find Billy's mum, but she still had one idea up her sleeve and this could be her last chance.

Thirty-Three

England, the present

Mandy was back. She looked terrible, and I hoped her dad was okay. I remembered my promise to be nicer after shouting at her in the car park when she thought she was protecting me from the purple Rolls Royce.

"It's good to see you back, Mandy," I said, using a friendly tone. "I hope your dad's okay."

Her reaction was not what I was expecting. "No Billy, Papa is bad. Very bad."

She sounded cross about it, and I felt sorry for her dad. I mean, he couldn't help feeling bad, could he?

I changed the subject and told her the news story about the Scottish island, so she didn't feel left out. I didn't tell her anything about the Russians because she's Russian and it might embarrass her. I hoped Frank wouldn't read the article. He's already rude to Mandy and would probably think the Russian in the paper was her dad or something!

I soon discovered Frank *had* read the article. In fact, he was more obsessed with the Russian story than I was, and kept asking for all the newspapers.

"Billy lad," he said. "'ave you seen this missile malarkey? Them blinkin' Ruskies up to no good as usual. Keep an eye on me medals would ya son?"

He still had his medals taped up across his jacket, and I couldn't see the connection between them and the missile, but disconnection at Autumn Days wasn't unusual.

"It's okay, Frank," I said. "The mystery of the missing shiny things has been solved. There haven't been any thefts for ages."

"If I fall asleep in me chair, would you keep an eye on them," he said. Then he lowered his voice so I could barely hear.

"If anything 'appens to me, make sure to take the chip out. Would you do that for me?"

"What chip?" I asked.

"The one in me medals," he said impatiently, as if I was being stupid. "These Ruskies with their missiles, they're giving me the heebie-jeebies. The chip is the antidote, so to speak. I can't say more than that," and he tapped his finger with his nose.

I didn't have a clue what Frank was talking about, and hoped his dementia wasn't getting worse.

Gran was half asleep. Her words had become very garbled since yesterday and she was even more difficult to understand than usual. I felt bad about what I was going to do, but I just *had* to know about Immerson. I checked to make sure Neelam wasn't near and then I said in a sort of conversational manner, "Gran, do you remember a man called Mr Immerson?"

Gran opened her eyes properly and looked at me. I was expecting her to get all excited again and was all ready to calm her down, but she just stared at me.

"Immerson." I repeated.

"Theran ice purkpyen dafidge," she said, nodding and smiling.

I was glad to hear Gran speaking without getting worked up all over again, and now I knew for sure that the name Immerson meant nothing to her. She was more concerned about a nice pork pie in the fridge.

Apart from showing Gran the photo again, I couldn't think of anything else to do, so I took a newspaper from the bin and opened it at the page with the photo of Mr Immerson.

I tapped Gran's arm and pointed to the photo. She grabbed my hand and started pointing too. "Immycale. Chook Immycale." she said, quite calmly.

Immycale. A new word, I was making progress.

"Gran," I said, "do you know that man?"

"Bah. Torso no im. Immerson!"

I grabbed a pen and a piece of paper and started writing down Gran's words.

"That's great Gran," I said. "Who is he?"

"Immerson Immycale!" she said. She was quite calm and if anything, she said these last two words almost proudly.

"Immerson?" I asked.

"Nooo. Im mer son!"

I wrote it all down.

"Immycale?" I asked, trying to sound out the word just as she had said it.

Gran nodded. I think she thought I had finally understood. I hadn't understood and I found it very frustrating. Suddenly,

I realised how much worse it would be if you were trying to talk to someone, and every time you said something that sounded perfectly clear to you, the person you were speaking to just looked at you blankly. Especially if it was something as important as the words Immerson and Immycale were to Gran.

Neelam came over and Gran held my hand, nodding at me. "Immycale," she said.

Neelam looked at me and whispered, "Do you know what she's saying?"

"Not yet," I whispered back. "I've written it down and I'm going to work it out."

I stayed with Gran and stared at the words. I made my eyes scrunch up. I read it upside down and backwards, but I just couldn't work it out.

Mandy brought us some of her home-made cookies.

"Billy, I need talk with you. Important something," she said.

I told her I just needed to sort out this thing with Gran first, then I'd come and find her. But I got so wrapped up in the Immerson puzzle, I forgot.

That night I lay in bed saying the words in my head. Breaking them into small pieces.

Torso no im. Chook. Im mer son. Im my cale

Torso? That means body. And chook is what chickens say. So Gran saw a chicken's body?

I started again.

I my cul? My cul .... Michael!

It's Michael! I'd got it! It's my dad!

It's my dad with a Russian arms dealer? Surely not.

I looked again at the other words. How could I have been so stupid? No wonder Gran was upset. She wasn't saying Immerson at all. She was saying, "It's my son!"

Tors o no im. She was saying, "Of course I know him! Chook. Look!"

Of course I know him. Look. It's my son. It's Michael!

I jumped out of bed and turned on my light. 2.07am. I couldn't wake up Neelam in the middle of the night, but I was far too excited to sleep.

My dad. My own dad. He was alive! What about my mum? Where was she? Had she been on the island? I grabbed the newspaper again to examine my dad's face. Did I look like him? I thought our eyes might be roughly the same shape, but the picture was too grainy to be certain.

How could my dad have anything to do with a Russian missile? Had he been kept there as a prisoner for eleven years? I had so many questions revolving around my head I didn't think I would ever sleep again, and I kept looking at the time to see when I could go to Neelam's room.

I messaged Louis to ask him to come ASAP, and he sent me a thumbs up. I waited until the clock finally showed 6.55, then I pulled on some clothes and rushed out of my room to look for Neelam. She wasn't in the lounge or in the kitchen. I ran to her flat and knocked on the door but there was no reply. Now what?

I turned to go back to my room and noticed Gran's door wasn't quite shut. I quietly pushed it open and there was Neelam sitting on Gran's bed.

Gran looked very tired. She was shaking her head and patting Neelam's hand.

"Neelam, Gran's been trying to tell us that the man in the news is my dad!"

"What? No Billy, I don't think your dad can be Russian."

"No, not Zoran, Mr Immerson. But he's not Immerson. Gran's been saying, *It's my son!*"

I brought out the photo again. "Gran, which one is Michael?"

She pointed at the one without a beard.

"Dat mycale," she said.

"I'm going to call Louis," said Neelam.

"You don't need to," I said. "He's already on his way."

I could hardly eat my scrambled egg, I was so excited. Mandy came to sit next to me. "Billy, important to talk now. Very important."

"What is it? Louis's coming. We might have found my dad."

"I find your Mama," she said. Well *that* made me listen.

"What? What did you say? My mum?"

"Come," she said, standing up. "Not here."

I followed Mandy to her room, worried that Louis might turn up at any minute, but needing to find out what Mandy had to say.

"In Moscow, my bad Papa has your Mama," she said. "She is, how to say, science person?"

"A scientist?" I suggested, forgetting about Louis for a moment.

"Yes, scientist," she said. "Papa took her, and I try find her, no find yet."

"Are you telling me *your* dad kidnapped *my* mum?" I asked, incredulously.

Mandy nodded, "So sorry, Billy. I get Mama home for you, I promise that. Please to tell no person. I need do this alone. Tell no person, okay?"

I didn't have time to reply because I could hear Louis's voice and Mandy hurried away.

"I was on a night shift, mate," said Louis. "Were you up all night?"

I nodded and went to get the photo. "Look, this one's my dad," I said, and told him how Gran had recognised him and how I'd worked out what she was saying.

"Wow, well-done mate, and well-done Gran," he said. "For her to have recognised your dad from such a poor-quality picture was a pretty good effort. Let's hope this is the breakthrough we've been waiting for. I called the police, and they're sending someone straight away. Not the usual guy I speak to, someone new has been put on the case. He'll be here soon."

Neelam appeared from her office. "The detective's here," she said. "He's waiting downstairs."

A detective! We went down in the lift, Gran in her wheelchair, to the private room where relatives can talk without being disturbed.

The detective wasn't what I expected. I assumed he'd look like one of those policemen you see on the TV wearing shades, or at least a leather jacket, but he wasn't cool at all. He had his hair stiffly gelled back and his light grey trousers were too short.

"D.C. Watham-Jones," he said, talking as if he had a table-tennis ball in his mouth. He shook hands with Louis and nodded at Neelam. He didn't even look at me or Gran.

"Now then, I understand someone has..."

"Excuse me," I said to DC Watham-Jones because I couldn't wait any longer. "Have they found out where Zoran went?"

DC Watham-Jones looked at me as if he hadn't noticed me before.

"And who might you be?" he asked in a condescending voice.

"I'm Billy, and that's my dad in the photo."

"I think you'll find that information hasn't been established yet," he said.

DC Watham-Jones was looking down his nose and talking through it in a way that made me want to hit it, but I felt Louis's hand on my back, so I thrust my clenched fists in my pockets and remained silent.

"Now then, who is the person who *thinks* she recognises a suspect?" said D.C. Watham-Jones.

"Hang on a minute," said Louis. "The man Gran recognised is *not* a suspect."

"We'll see," said D.C. Watham-Jones with a smirk.

I wished they'd sent a different detective, this wasn't going well.

He held up a black zipped folder and took out some photos. He placed them on the table in front of Gran, and Neelam gave Gran her glasses. I felt a bit tense because it was so important that Gran should recognise my dad again, but she was more interested in the detective's yellow tie.

"Well?" said D.C. Watham-Jones to Neelam, as if there was no point asking Gran herself, "Does she recognise anyone?"

I went round the table to have a closer look at the photos. They weren't the same as the photo in the paper and they weren't as clear. I could see five men, although I couldn't be sure if they were the same five men.

"Gran," I said. "Can you see Michael?"

Gran looked at me and smiled. Then she pointed at me and said, "Michael!"

"No Gran, I'm Billy. Can you see Michael in the photos?"

"This is pointless," said Watham-Jones. "She can't even recognise her own grandson. How can anyone expect her to pick out a man she hasn't seen for eleven years."

"Detective Constable Watham-Jones," said Neelam in her calm voice, which always meant trouble. "Gran recognised the man in the news photographs on several occasions. If you want further assistance from her you will need to find some better photographs." And with that she wheeled Gran out of the room.

Louis and I looked at each other. It was a disaster, but we hadn't seen all the photos. There were plenty more in his folder.

"Could we see the other photos please?" I asked.

"You can have a look, although you won't find anything of significance," said Watham-Jones, handing them to Louis.

Louis gave me a pile and we both started looking through. Most of the photos were of burnt-out buildings, a couple were of a path which seemed to be heading towards a beach and quite a few were scraps of paper with writing on them.

There was nothing of interest and we'd both had enough. We left DC Watham-Jones talking on his phone and decided to go outside for some fresh air. I noticed a tall, foreign-looking man, wearing a long black coat getting out of a flashy silver Mercedes. I didn't recognise him and briefly wondered who he was visiting, but Louis was already marching out of the car park, and I had to run to catch him up. We didn't speak at all until we were sitting on the bench that looks out over the lake.

"I'm sorry mate, we didn't get anywhere, did we?" said Louis.

The lake was the same as usual and so were all the people in the park. A little girl was feeding the ducks with her mum. There were joggers, cyclists and walkers. I wished we'd just come to play football, and everything was back to normal.

"Louis," I began. "That photo, Gran definitely recognised my dad."

"I know," said Louis.

"Do you think he's in Russia?"

"I'm afraid it looks that way."

It was hopeless. Dad had been taken to Russia and mum... I needed to get back to talk to Mandy!

"Shall we go back?" asked Louis. "There must be something we can do to find your dad."

We stood up to leave and I hoped the idiot Watham-Jones wouldn't still be at home.

"I hope that idiot Wally-Jones isn't still there," said Louis, which made me laugh.

Thirty-Four

England, the present

Manya woke up, back at Autumn Days, wishing the last twenty-four hours had been a dream. More like a nightmare. Admittedly, she had enjoyed using her judo techniques on Tatiana and driving Papa's Mercedes of course. But having been tricked by Tatiana yet again, she'd driven straight to the airport and taken the first flight back to England. The journey had given her time to reflect. Finding that her father had been the person responsible for kidnapping Billy's mum was a terrible discovery, and now it was up to her to put things right.

Putting things right partly depended on how much Papa needed Manya back in Russia. If he wanted his daughter badly enough, she might have some bargaining power.

Right now she needed to find Billy, and went out to clear away the breakfast, hoping to find him on his own. She wanted to tell him his mum was in Russia. Not safe perhaps, but alive.

A newspaper had been left on the table with the name Zoran Krasnov standing out in large black letters. Zoran. Where had she heard that name recently?

"Zoran is waiting," the thin woman in Papa's office had said. How common was the name Zoran? Could she have been talking about the same man?

She rushed back to her room with the paper, ignoring the reaction from Gordon, the chef, who made a comment about Manya thinking she was still on holiday.

She turned on her phone to find more about Zoran, and a new photo came up. This time she recognised the face. *I've seen that man before, but where?* she asked herself. That heavy beard, those deep-set eyes, the thick eyebrows.

She didn't have time to think because a stream of messages came through from her father.

Manya, where are you? I'm waiting in my office.

The message had been sent the day before. Then, *What did you do to Tatiana?* Followed by, *Have you taken my car? What's going on?* And finally, late last night, *Manya, where are you?*

Was he worried about her? More likely he was worried about his car. She was ashamed of her father, of what he had done, and she didn't care if he was worried. He'd caused plenty of worry himself.

Manya, in no hurry to reply, turned her attention back to the photo of Zoran, trying to remember where she'd seen him before. Not in Moscow on her recent visit, she was sure about that. He hadn't been involved with her training, or school. No, she needed to go back further.

She closed her eyes and took herself back to that terrible night of the fire. The memory she'd buried for so long. Her father had taken her on the plane, and he'd been shouting at someone. A man with dark hair, deep-set eyes and thick eyebrows. It was Zoran! Zoran had been involved with the kidnapping too.

She went to find Billy, but he was sitting with Gran, and Manya couldn't get him to listen without drawing attention to herself.

In desperation, she went back to her room to send a message to her father.

Papa, you must send Billy's mum home.

There was no response.

Manya spent a sleepless night trying to work out the link between her father, Billy's parents, Zoran, the telescope and the missile, but she couldn't find any connections.

In the morning there was still no message. Had Tatiana told Mr Molchalin about their fight? Had she convinced him that Manya wasn't worth the trouble? She hoped not.

The most important thing now was to talk to Billy, but he, Louis and Neelam were involved in some sort of meeting.

She couldn't wait in her room, she had to do something, so she ran downstairs again, planning to wait for the meeting to finish, but the door was open and Billy wasn't there. Glancing out through the front door, she could see Billy and Louis walking away from Autumn Days, and was about to run after them when a tall, dark, familiar figure appeared, striding towards the front door. She froze.

What was he doing here? Why had he come?

She turned and ran up the stairs in time to hear the phone ringing in Neelam's office. The call would be to announce the arrival of her father.

Gordon was passing and picked up the receiver, "Yes, she's up here," he said into the phone, "Mandy, there's someone in reception asking for you. It's a Mr Molchalin."

Now she understood why he hadn't responded to her message, he'd been on his way to England! He'd come to take her back to Russia. She must *not* go down to him, she was safer up here where he wouldn't be able to force her to go with him.

Her only option was to invite her father to come upstairs, and she asked Gordon to show him which way to go.

As if in a trance, Manya wandered back to her room. She straightened the chairs, the cushions and her photos.

"Babushka, I really need your help," she said to the image of her grandmother.

There was a knock at the door and Manya went to open it.

"Manya, what happened? Why did you leave?" asked Mr Molchalin, closing the door behind him.

Manya ushered her father into the room and motioned for him to sit down.

"Manya, you need to know the truth, then you will understand why you must come home. You will *want* to come home."

Manya nodded and sat down.

"When I met your mother, she was a smart girl, straight out of school. She had no ambitions other than to look pretty, get married and have lots of children. I was a few years older and needed a wife who was willing to stay at home, accompany me to business functions and start what I hoped would become a Molchalin dynasty. Your mother was perfect. She even came with a willing cook and baby-sitter."

"Babushka." said Manya, softly.

"That's right," continued Mr Molchalin. "After you were born, your mother was not able to have more children. She was devastated, yet I could see, from the day you were born, that you were a fighter. You kicked and screamed your way through the first few weeks of life, and you became my protégé. I didn't need a dynasty, all I needed was a child of my own who could learn from me, and eventually take over the successful business I was building.

"You showed so much promise, Manya, you were everything I could have hoped for. Then you began to have your own ideas and started drifting away from me. You just didn't have the same vision as me. But I wasn't discouraged. I believed your strong will could be shaped and I could lead you to the destiny I had always planned."

Manya wanted to cover her ears and run away. Had her father really been controlling her life all along? She looked at Babushka's face smiling at her out of the photograph.

"You need to be strong. You can do anything you set your mind to," she had said.

I'm not strong, thought Manya, *I've done exactly what Papa wanted. I'm a weak, worthless puppet, completely under his control since the day I was born.*

Mr Molchalin's voice interrupted her thoughts.

"That was when I asked Tatiana to help me. It was Tatiana who guided you through your training and showed you the importance of serving the Motherland. And in serving the Motherland we can make the name Molchalin great, Manya. We are so similar, can't you see?"

"No, Papa," said Manya, finding her voice. "I can't see. I would never take parents away from their child. I would never blackmail them the way you have blackmailed Billy's mum. I'm not ruthless like you."

"What are you talking about?" said Mr Molchalin. "Whose parents am I supposed to have blackmailed?"

"Billy's parents!" cried Manya.

Mr Molchalin looked genuinely nonplussed. "I'm sorry, Manya, I have no idea what you are talking about."

"I know it was you," persisted Manya, trying to stay calm. "You made me go with you that night when you set fire to Billy's house."

Mr Molchalin looked at his daughter, a slow realisation appearing on his face. "There was a child?" he asked, his voice almost a whisper.

"Yes, there was a child. Billy is the son of Galileo." She paused, watching the confusion on her father's face. "Do you even know what I've been doing in England?"

"Of course. Tatiana arranged for you to spend time here to improve your spoken English," he said.

"Tatiana has been lying to you," said Manya.

"No, Manya, you are mistaken. Tatiana is totally trustworthy and she's ready to welcome you at DM Engineering. Come back to Moscow with me now, Manya. Let's sort this out back at home, we can work together. You will run the business alongside me and live at Villa Molchalin!"

"I'm not coming to Russia with you, Papa! I'm staying here in England with my friends."

Mr Molchalin stood up. "In that case I will have to..."

There was a light knock at the door and Manya quickly went to open it, thankful for the interruption.

"Mandy, here you are! I've *got* to talk with you *right now*, it's really important."

Billy walked into the room, faltered for a moment, and then held out his hand to her father.

"Oh hello," he said. "I'm Billy."

Thirty-Five

England, the present

When we got back to Autumn Days, I went straight to find Mandy.

She wasn't in the kitchen, so I quickly walked to her room and knocked on the door. Mandy opened it, but she wasn't alone. The man I'd seen earlier in the car park, getting out of the silver Mercedes, was standing there. I didn't know what to do or say, so I stuck out my hand and shook his.

"Hello, I'm Billy," I said.

The man didn't introduce himself, he just looked surprised. He said something to Mandy in Russian, which made me think he might be Mandy's dad. Was this the man who'd kidnapped my mum?

"Have you got my mum?" I asked.

He gave me an odd look, slightly puzzled, and left the room.

"What about Mum?" I asked Mandy, feeling panicky. "Is he going to send her back?"

Mandy looked at me. "Billy, I try to get her home. I try always until she comes."

I couldn't stand it. I had to speak with the man who might be Mandy's dad to find out what he'd done with my mum. I wasn't thinking straight. If I had, I would never have run after him.

I only just made it. The big Russian had already got into the back of the Mercedes when I rushed up and pulled the door open.

"I want my mum back!" I said. "I know you've got her."

He looked surprised to see me. "You are Billy?" he asked in his heavy Russian accent.

I nodded and stood holding the door, so the driver couldn't leave. This might be the only chance to get Mum back and I wasn't going to waste it.

He stared at me for a moment, as if he was thinking about something, maybe making a plan.

"Come. We talk in the car."

I didn't hesitate. I got into the car beside this Russian who I already knew to be a bit dodgy. What was I thinking of? Neelam and Louis had told me a thousand times not to go with a stranger, and I was doing something even worse. I hadn't even told them I was going. I had no coat, no phone, no money. I knew it was reckless, but what choice did I have? If there was even a slim chance this man could lead me to Mum, I had to take it.

The driver looked concerned. "You coming too then, lad?" he asked.

"Drive," the Russian said, pressing a button. A glass screen slowly rose out from a black panel behind the driver, cutting off the sound between the front and back of the car.

"Tell me, Billy, why do you live in this care home," he asked.

I told him about the fire and my parents being kidnapped, thinking he must know all about it if he'd done the kidnapping, but he seemed shocked. His head kept changing direction, nodding at some of the things I told him, shaking at others.

Eventually, when I'd finished, he shut his eyes and didn't speak. Either he was being incredibly rude, or he was thinking. I hoped he was thinking.

After about five minutes of sitting in silence, with just the hum of the car's engine and the faint sound of Classic FM drifting through from the front of the car, the Russian opened his eyes and looked at me.

"We go to Moscow. I help you find your mother. Maybe then Manya will return.."

I wanted to ask who Manya was, but it was an insignificant point if he was going to take me to Mum. Instead, I asked, "How are we going to get there"

"My private jet is waiting."

A private jet!

So, instead of thinking logically, I went with him. All I could think about was rescuing Mum. Single-mindedly and single-handedly.

The Russian didn't speak to me again for the rest of the car journey. He kept tapping his knee with his fingers, as though thinking about something important. Or maybe he was in a hurry. I thought it was best to stay quiet as I didn't want him to change his mind about taking me.

It gave me plenty of time to think about what I was doing. My mind kept flitting between hope and fear. Hope that I was on my way to rescue Mum. Fear that even if this was the man who'd kidnapped her, he wasn't going to just hand her over because I'd been brave - or perhaps stupid - enough to get into the car with him. My sweaty palms and the constant prickle across my back suggested fear was gaining the upper hand.

I'd never flown before, so I didn't know what to expect, but when the driver turned down a long driveway and a huge silver space-age building loomed in front of us, I knew this was no ordinary airport. Small planes were lined up in neat rows. Each one was gleaming as though it had just come off the production line, and the aircraft hangars behind them looked like some enormous, wavy work of art.

I noticed the other cars: Ferraris, Porsches and Lamborghinis. This was a strange new world. At that moment I wasn't scared anymore, I was spellbound, and didn't mind at all waiting in the car while he, "attended to some important business", because there was so much to see.

"Don't worry about the paperwork," he said when he came back to the car. "I have some useful friends." I hadn't thought about the problem of travelling without a passport up until that point. I wasn't sure if he really did have influential friends, or if he'd just bribed someone. Whichever it was, it meant that two hours later, I was on board the private jet, sipping a tall glass of orange juice and gazing out at the extraordinary spectacle beneath me. It was like zooming out on Google Maps in slow motion, but better because things were moving. Tiny cars, ripples on the sea, wispy clouds.

I nearly choked on my orange juice when I suddenly remembered I hadn't told anyone where I was going. I hadn't considered how worried Neelam might be. I hadn't thought about how Louis, Katie and Mandy would be out looking for me. I hadn't even thought about Gran.

"Would it be possible for me to call Neelam and tell her I'm with you?" I said.

"How old are you?" he asked, unexpectedly.

"Fourteen."

"Hmm, I know a boy the same age in Russia," he said, looking slightly less fierce. "He likes football. Do you?"

"Yes," I said, "I'm a Spurs fan." I felt better talking about something normal like football, but that didn't mean Neelam would feel better. I was imagining her phoning Katie, calling the police, and generally panicking.

"I think Neelam's going to be worried," I said.

"It is not possible for you to make contact with England," said the Russian.

What did he mean? Couldn't you use a phone in a private jet? Or had I just allowed myself to be kidnapped by someone pretending to be Mandy's dad and who might not be her dad after all? Maybe he was Zoran!

"Can I ask you one thing?" I asked. "Are you Mandy's dad?"

The Russian looked at me, frowning and shaking his head. "Mandy? Who is Mandy? I am Dmitri Molchalin, head of DM Engineering."

I sat back in my seat and looked out of the window, but the view had disappeared. It had suddenly become black outside, and I felt black inside too.

What on earth had I let myself in for?

By the time we landed, I'd made up my mind to go along with Mr Molchalin's plan, whatever it was. I didn't have much choice. The police in England hadn't done a very good job finding my parents for the last eleven years, and now, if Mr Molchalin was telling the truth about helping me to get Mum back, I needed to get this right.

It was freezing and still dark as I walked down the steps from the plane. I had some idea from geography that Russia was ahead of England so, according to my watch, it must be nearly midnight. Another Mercedes was waiting to collect us, this time a black one. I was glad to get straight into the warm car, but I couldn't stop shivering. Mr Molchalin spoke to the driver. He must have been explaining why I was with him because the driver kept looking at me. He didn't look friendly.

We drove through a city which was still busy with people who'd been out for the evening. There were bright lights and, apart from the strange writing, I thought we could be in any city, anywhere in the world, but I guessed we were in Moscow because the word 'Moskva' kept popping up. Mr Molchalin spoke constantly on his phone, and I couldn't understand anything he said except for one word which he kept repeating: Galileo. He sounded very angry.

After a while, as we left the lights behind and drove along a dark, narrow road, I suddenly felt very tired. Sinking back into the seat I felt my eyes begin to droop.

The car finally stopped outside a big building with lights shining out of plant pots and a smart-looking man wearing a suit standing by the front door.

"You will rest here tonight," said Mr Molchalin. "I will come for you in the morning."

I wanted to ask about Mum, ask if I could send a message to Neelam, but my body and my brain both felt like jelly, and the thought of sleeping in a bed was too inviting. The smart man held the door open, as I followed Mr Molchalin into the hotel. A woman sitting behind a desk smiled at me and handed me some keys as though she'd been expecting me. Another woman appeared from nowhere and told me to follow her, and when I turned around, Mr Molchalin had gone. The woman took me up in a lift and showed me to a bedroom. The lights were already on, and I entered a room with a big double bed, a white chest of drawers, and a door leading into a small bathroom. A pair of blue pyjamas was laid out on the bed, and a pile of clothes sat neatly on a chair.

The woman shut the curtains and left me. I slipped on the pyjamas, got into the huge bed and, not having slept for a couple of nights, fell asleep almost immediately.

Thirty-Six

England, the present

Manya watched helplessly, as Billy spoke to her father.

"Have you got my mum?" he asked.

Her father, for once, didn't know how to respond. Instead, he turned to her.

"Manya, come with me. You belong at DM Engineering, it's your destiny."

"After all your lies, why would I want to help you? How could you let Tatiana take control of me? As soon as you leave, I'm going to destroy this phone, then neither of you will have any hold over me at all."

Manya threw the phone on the bed. She would have liked to crush it on the floor in front of her father, but without it, her investigations would be impossible. She wasn't going to give up on Billy's mum, although returning to Russia with her father was out of the question. She would never be able to trust him again.

And yet he appeared to be genuinely surprised that Galileo had a child. Had he really not known about Billy, or about the reason for her residence in England? If he was telling the truth, it meant Tatiana had been lying to him, and that raised further questions about her loyalty and agenda. Had she been deliberately withholding information, manipulating both of them? What would Tatiana gain from hiding Billy's existence from Papa?

What was Tatiana up to?

There was no time to reflect on Tatiana's intentions because after Mr Molchalin's abrupt departure, Billy had also slipped out of the room.

Manya retrieved the phone from the bed and sent a message to her father.

Please send Galileo home. You don't need her now, Billy does.

Now that Papa had met Billy, surely he would have some sympathy.She thought back over their conversation. Why would Tatiana have lied to him? What was Zoran's involvement and why was her father in a meeting with him? It didn't make sense.

"Mandy," came Neelam's voice from outside her door.

"Mandy, are you in there? Have you seen Billy?"

Manya opened her door, a sense of alarm rising. "He was here since half an hour, I don't know where is he now."

Billy had left soon after her father. Mr Molchalin was taller and probably stronger than Billy, but he couldn't have abducted him in full view of everyone could he? It would be impossible, Billy would have got away easily. No, there had to be another explanation.

"We don't want to upset anyone," said Neelam. "So we're being careful not to say too much to the residents. Could you help look for him?

"Of course," said Manya, grabbing her jacket and phone.

As she rushed through the lounge, she heard Frank's voice, "It's the blinkin' Rusky," he said. "She's got Billy. She's probably got 'is parents an' all!"

"Stop that right now, Frank," came Beryl's voice. "You've got to stop thinking every foreign person is out to get us."

Manya didn't hear any more. She was already down the stairs, heading for the exit. What Frank had said was true, she was the "blinkin' Rusky" involved in the kidnappings, and now she was going to put things right.

She ran to Katie's house and pounded on the door. "I am Mandy, friend Billy. I need speak with Katie please," she said, breathlessly.

"Katie's not here," said her mum. "She's at hockey training. Are you okay?" Katie's mum looked worried.

"Please you ask her calling me," said Manya.

"Is something wrong?" Katie's mum called after her, but Manya was already on her way to Jude's house. He was the only other person who might have seen Billy. She ran slowly through the park, checking all the benches and other places where Billy might have gone to be alone, but the park was nearly empty. She ran down the alleyway, remembering how she'd dealt with Jude and his gang. Jude wasn't going to want to help her, but he was her last hope.

A woman wearing a dressing gown and hair curlers came to the door. Before Manya could speak, she was calling up the stairs.

"Jude, it's another girly for ya. Watchit, ya don't want to end up like that sleaze-bag dad a yours. One at a time, atta boy."

Manya had no idea what the woman was talking about, so she smiled and said, "Thank you. It is important."

"Foreign bird this time," Jude's mum called up.

Jude appeared at the top of the stairs, took one look at Manya and disappeared. "Please Yude," Manya called up the stairs. "Billy is gone. Maybe kidnapped, I need know if you see him."

Jude came down the stairs. "Who'd kidnap Billy?" he asked. "It wasn't me, if that's what you're asking."

"No, not you, bad Russians. Please look for him, Yude. Call my number if you finding him."

"Giving 'er number now, pushy little miss," said Jude's mum.

Thirty-Seven

Moscow, the present

I was woken by an alarm and, opening my eyes, tried to remember where I was. The ringing continued, and I realised it was coming from a phone next to the bed. I picked it up.

"Good morning, Billy," came a woman's voice. "Your car will be outside in half an hour. Be ready, you have a long day ahead."

That was all she said. I checked my watch which said 05.00. That would be English time, so it was still quite early in Russia, if that's where I was.

I took a quick shower and looked at the pile of clothes on the chair. There was a red and blue tracksuit with an embroidered red, gold and blue logo: UCSK. I knew that Russian football team. Cool.

There were still twenty minutes to wait, and I hoped to find some breakfast downstairs. I was starving, not having eaten since lunchtime the day before. Outside the door was a trolley laden with food.

Wheeling it into the room, I threw one of the tiny rolls into my mouth before I'd even sat down. Everything looked and smelled so good I hardly knew where to start. The blinis looked just like the ones Mandy made - little pancakes with strawberry jam and cream on top. I glugged down a glass of pink fruit juice and then tasted the porridge, which was too thick and salty, so I moved onto the eggs which had some funny orange fishy stuff on them. Then, just as I was about to start on the sausages, the phone rang again.

"Your car is waiting outside," a voice said.

I wrapped the sausages in a paper napkin and stuffed them into the rucksack which had been left next to the clothes, alongside a jacket with a furry lining and I put that on too. Things were looking good.

Feeling much better than the night before, I stepped out of the lift into a classy hallway which I'd been too tired to notice the night before. Gold mirrors, marble pillars and uncomfortable-looking armchairs gave a good impression of the hotel in 'To Catch a Thief', one of the films the Oldies watch all the time. In fact, my whole situation felt surreal, and I was half-expecting to wake up at home. I didn't want to wake up. The day ahead was completely out of my control, but if I focused on Mum, on taking her home, I would be able to hold it together. The woman at the desk by the entrance nodded and smiled, so I gave her a cheery wave as I left. "I'm rescuing my mum today," I said. She looked confused, but I didn't care whether she understood or not.

With a renewed sense of optimism, I marched through the hotel's revolving front door, out into the cold morning air where reality hit me. Seeing Mr Molchalin waiting for me was what I was expecting, but not entirely what I wanted. It would have been so much easier if he could have delivered Mum to the hotel and sent us home together. I gritted my teeth, threw my new rucksack onto the back seat of the same black Mercedes as the night before, and climbed into the passenger seat, next to the big Russian who was sitting at the wheel.

"I hope you slept well," he said.

"Yes thanks," I replied in a voice that sounded far more confident than I felt. "And thanks for the new gear - CSKA Moscow, right?"

"Correct," he said.

"Are we going to get Mum now?" I asked.

"Soon, but you must play your part of the deal first."

This was a major blow, and I could see how sharp the Russian was. He'd got me on side with the tracksuit, the coat and the breakfast, but it didn't mean he was about to go easy on me. I was way out of my depth.

"Hold it," I said, determined not to be out-manoeuvred. "Why would I trust you? You took my mum. I need proof you'll send her home before I co-operate."

The Russian laughed. "You certainly have courage," he said. "But now, you must trust me."

Thirty-Eight
England, the present

Manya spent most of the night trying to get in touch with her father.

Have you taken Billy?

Are you back in Moscow?

Billy is missing. Papa, please tell me if you know where he is.

Please Papa.

No response.

The only message was from Katie, asking what was going on. Manya messaged back to ask if Katie had seen Billy, but hope was dwindling.

Neelam hadn't slept either. Her eyes were red-rimmed, and her usually tidy, smooth hair was a mess. Both she and Louis were sitting in Neelam's office, talking urgently on their phones. The atmosphere was unbearably tense and Manya decided it might be best not to disturb them.

Gordon was dealing with breakfast.

"Terrible situation isn't it?" he said. "That poor boy. First he loses his parents, then he takes himself off all alone. I wish he'd just pick up his phone and let Neelam know where he is, she's beside herself. Do you know what's going on?"

"No," said Manya. "I am looking all the time until he comes home."

"Was that your dad here yesterday?" asked Gordon.

Manya didn't know how to answer. She didn't want to lie, but she didn't want Neelam or Louis to know her father had been there, at Autumn Days.

"He was visitor from my country, Russia," she said, before grabbing a couple of plates and escaping from the kitchen, away from Gordon's questions. Frank and Beryl were sitting together as she put the toast on the table.

"You bin spyin' on us?" asked Frank. "What've ya done with our Billy?"

Manya didn't reply. Time was running out for her, for Billy and for Billy's parents. She went to her room and took her phone out of her pocket, hoping to see a new message.

Nothing from her father.

She stood with her head pressed against the bedroom wall, wondering what to do. It looked increasingly likely that her father had taken Billy, but why would he do that and how could she reach him?

"Mandy, can I come in?" Neelam was at the door and Manya rushed to open it. "Has he been found?" she asked.

"No," said Neelam. "Mandy, I'm so sorry to have to ask you this, but Gordon said you had a visitor yesterday."

"Yes, I did," replied Manya.

"Well, Gordon said your visitor left looking angry, and Billy went missing soon after. Do you mind if I ask who the visitor was?"

"It was my father."

"And is there any chance at all he might know where Billy is?"

By mid-morning there was still no news. Manya had convinced Neelam that her father couldn't possibly have seen where Billy went. He didn't even *know* Billy.

A policeman had arrived at Autumn Days and taken statements from everyone, including all the residents. DC Watham-Jones had upset everybody with his direct questioning and unsubtle suggestions. Gran had been reduced to tears, Frank was furious because he thought he was being accused of kidnap, and Pasqual had admitted to the detective that he and Beryl were alien imposters about to be beamed up to their spaceship.

Manya was relieved the policeman was taking so long, it gave her a chance to get on with her own investigations. Katie had sent another message, asking what she could do to help.

Get friends and look for Billy, she messaged back. After all, there was a chance he was still in England. A very slim chance.

Neelam came to tell Manya that DC Watham-Jones had asked to speak with her. She followed Neelam into the office where the Detective Constable was waiting.

"Ah, so this is Mandy, our Russian friend," began DC Watham-Jones.

Manya didn't speak, so he continued in a pompous and condescending voice. "Can you explain why you are in England at this present moment in time?"

"I cook for residents," said Manya.

"I see," said Watham-Jones, taking notes. "And how long have you currently been living in this country?" He spoke loudly as though Manya might not understand unless he raised his voice.

Manya answered his questions. She desperately wanted to get back to her room to find out if her father had responded, but she didn't dare ask to leave because she couldn't think of a good enough excuse.

Eventually, the detective let her go and she rushed to her room and grabbed her phone.

Finally, a message from Papa. Manya opened it warily, hoping for an explanation, expecting a string of demands.

It wasn't the message she was expecting.

Thirty-Nine

Moscow, the present

The black Mercedes made its way through whichever city we were in, and I tried very hard not to let my thoughts wander away from the task in hand. I was so far in over my head I could hardly breathe, and yet this was my chance, possibly my only chance to save Mum. I had to stay calm and I had to make the right choices.

I made the wrong choice. Sitting in the car, it suddenly occurred to me that the man I was sitting with must surely be the man I'd seen in the newspaper, and he'd made up a false name to confuse me.

"You're Zoran aren't you!" I blurted out.

"No, I am not Zoran!" came the response which was so immediate and violent it made me jump. "I told you, I am Dmitri Molchalin." Mr Molchalin was gripping the steering wheel so tightly his knuckles had turned white. His face, on the other hand, had turned purple and looked ready to explode, the veins in his neck were bulging and his eyes were narrowed. I got the impression he didn't like Zoran.

Whether he was Zoran or Dmitri, it didn't matter. What mattered was that he had something to do with the disappearance of my parents.

"Well, why did you kidnap my parents, Dmitri Molchalin?" I asked angrily. I couldn't allow this bully to see my fear. I wasn't going to cave in at this point.

"It is a very complicated story," he replied. "I don't feel the need to explain myself to you, when you are the one who requires my help. You can just be proud that your mama has been part of a very successful project."

"Didn't you think my mum might not have wanted to be part of it?" I said. "That maybe she would have preferred to stay in England with her family. That having her house burnt down wasn't high on her list of priorities?"

"Some things in life, Billy, are more important than our own selfish desires," said the hypocrite. "What I have created, with the help of your mama, of course, is a work of genius. We have championed human progress and we will leave a positive footprint on the world."

"Oh yeah?" I said. "You're the one with the selfish desires, not me. I just wanted a normal life with my parents. What've you done to make the world a better place? You haven't made it better for *me*."

Mr Molchalin turned back to the road, and although he was driving, I saw his shoulders slump. He spoke in a whisper.

"I didn't know Galileo had a child. I didn't know she was still working here," he said.

So Mum was the Galileo he'd been talking about, but alarm bells were clanging inside my head.

"You didn't know? You didn't know Mum was still working for you? How can I take her back if you don't know where she is?"

"Billy, I know where she is. Trust me."

Trust him? The man made no sense. How could I trust him? The sweaty palms were back, and I began to wonder if I should make a run for it as soon as the car stopped.

We pulled up at the entrance to a building which was mostly glass with a big sign outside which I couldn't read because of the weird letters. I didn't have a chance to run because a man wearing a black suit and dark glasses opened the door for me and made it clear that my only option was to follow Mr Molchalin through swing doors, into an even more extravagant lobby than the one at the hotel. Its wooden floor was laid out in a spiral pattern, swinging chairs dangled down from the ceiling and, at the edges of the walls, tall green ferns, spiky cacti and yellow flowers sprouted from massive clay pots. This was his world, not mine, and it made me feel small and insignificant.

A receptionist wearing a red jacket looked at me curiously, as though I wasn't what she was expecting. She smiled widely at Mr Molchalin, but he was already striding towards the lift.

"Is Mum here?" I asked as the doors closed behind me. I didn't like being shut in a confined space with this man.

"Be patient," he said.

"What's this thing I have to do for you? The bit where I fulfil my part of the deal," I asked.

"Just a small thing," said Mr Molchalin. "A simple photo, that's all."

Despite the fact that my nervousness had reached a level where I fully expected to spontaneously combust at any moment, I couldn't help noticing the view. A wide river snaked through the city, dotted with boats and spanned by tall, arching bridges. An enormous red building pointed skywards, surrounded by an extraordinary huddle of skyscrapers. One looked as though it had been wrung out like a sponge and left twisted and broken.

Coming out of the lift, I noticed an open door. Sitting at a desk was someone with short, blond, spiky hair, but I couldn't tell if it was a man or a woman, because they had their head down.

Mr Molchalin's office had a massive window where I stood staring out at the incredible spectacle while he spoke in Russian on his phone.

After a few minutes, he finished talking and came to stand next to me.

"You like the view of Moscow?" he asked.

So I was right, we were in Moscow.

"And now this photo," he continued. "A selfie, I think you call it, of you and me smiling in front of the window."

If that was all I had to do, I could certainly manage a smile, even if it was a false one.

"Perfect," he said.

"What's it for?"

"Proof that you were here. Here through choice."

He sat down for a moment to send the photo.

It was yet another thing that didn't make sense, but before I could ask who he'd sent the photo to, Mr Molchalin told me to wait in his office for a few moments and not to touch anything.

He shut the door behind him, but I opened it and saw him go into the room with the spiky-haired person. He shut that door too and a big argument began. I couldn't understand what they were saying, of course, but the anger in their voices was unmistakable.

I shut the door again and went back to the window, trying to focus on the view rather than what the big row was about.

After what seemed like forever, Mr Molchalin returned, carrying a bunch of keys. He was talking on his phone and his tone had changed. He seemed happy, and actually smiled at me.

"That was Manya," he said, putting his phone in his jacket pocket. "She's coming home."

"Who's Manya?" I asked.

"Manya," he repeated. "Manya, my daughter. She has been living with you in the care home."

"D'you mean Mandy?" I asked. Even as I said it, I realised Mandy and Manya must be the same person.

"She must think a good deal of you, Billy," he continued. "She says she will return as soon as she sees you with your mama, safely back in England."

Go Mandy! I thought, suddenly feeling a lot more hopeful. *Frank's going to have a surprise when I tell him the Rusky's the one who clinched the deal. Not that I was going to play down my own part in this whole adventure. After all, it was me doing the difficult and scary stuff.*

"So what are we waiting for?" I asked. "Where's Mum?"

Another trip in the black Mercedes and another tour of Moscow took us to a very different part of the city. We must have crossed the river at least twice more, before arriving in a dilapidated area where the buildings were wide, flat and mostly made of corrugated metal.

The driver took us around to the front of one of the buildings and Mr Molchalin led me into a smartish hallway. Nothing to compare with the lobby of the posh skyscraper we'd just left, but better than I expected considering the decrepit building.

The noise was deafening. Through a window I could see below to an enormous, brightly lit underground room which stretched away out of sight. It was filled with machinery and people wearing white coats, hard hats and yellow gloves. Some of the machines were huge, with automatic levers hauling up vast sheets of curved metal. Others were small, a bit like microscopes with men and women peering into them.

Mr Molchalin wasn't happy about me looking through the window and guided me away from it towards a large white door. He took out the bunch of keys I'd seen earlier and fumbled about, trying to find the right fit. I got the impression this wasn't somewhere he visited often.

"Is Mum in here?" I asked. I wanted him to say yes, but I didn't want to think that Mum had been a prisoner here, locked behind the white door with this terrible noise almost shaking the flimsy building.

Eventually, the door opened and Mr Molchalin, ignoring my question, pushed me into another large room, this time dimly lit. Men and women wearing headsets, possibly to block out the noise, were concentrating in their own little booths, staring into double-screened computers.

I walked forward slowly, my eyes darting around the room, desperate to see that one familiar face. The walls seemed to close in on me as I came to the booth of a small, blond lady whose hair was scraped back into a ponytail. Could this be her? There was something very familiar about the tilt of her head, but this wasn't the time to make a mistake. This was a moment I'd been dreaming about for as long as I could remember.

She had coloured notes plastered all over the sides of her cubicle and I walked closer.

It felt like I'd been punched in the stomach. They weren't notes at all, they were photos.

Photos of me!

Nothing could stop me now. I took the final two steps which separated me and my mum. Eleven years we'd been apart, and as she turned, the years melted away. It was Mum, it was my actual mum and I was three again.

"Mum!" was all I could manage, my voice sounding croaky.

Her eyes adjusted to the light, she frowned for a moment and then stood up and grabbed my shoulders, scrutinising my face, her own face reflecting her disbelief.

"Billy?" she whispered.

I nodded.

"Billy, is it you? Billy, is this really you?"

"Yes, Mum, it's me! It's really me! I've found you and I've come to take you home!"

Tears were welling up inside me, and Mum's eyes, which had seemed so lifeless when she'd first turned around, suddenly lit up.

She flung her arms around me, clinging to me as though I might disappear if she let go.

I don't know how long we stood together like that, but eventually Mr Molchalin came over to us and Mum spoke to him in Russian.

My mum can speak Russian!

A few hours later, Mum and I were flying back to England on Mr Molchalin's private jet. It had all happened very quickly, almost as though he couldn't wait to be rid of us. I would have been happy if the flight had gone around the world ten times. There was so much I wanted to ask Mum, but there was even more she wanted to ask me.

Once I'd filled her in on my past eleven years, at least the basics, she began to tell me what had happened to her.

When she was in England, she'd been working on a top-secret project to create a telescope which could see into black holes, but after a while, strange things began to happen and Mum became aware of suspicious activity. Someone was following her and she didn't know why, until one day, a message popped up on her computer screen which said she must go to a certain place that evening or she would never see her little boy again. That was me.

Not having any idea where the message had come from, she and Dad decided their best immediate action would be to pack up and leave. They took their essentials and drove to a remote village much further south, where they'd rented a house while they worked out what to do next.

"It was a stupid move," said Mum. "I should have reported it straightaway, but I didn't know if the message had come internally or externally. I was so scared for you and Gran, I just wanted to get away. Far away."

"So they followed you?" I said.

"They must have done. We didn't tell anyone where we were going, and that was stupid too. I've had eleven years to regret that decision."

"What happened?" I asked.

"That night," said Mum, "we'd just managed to get you to bed when there was a massive crash in the kitchen. The next thing I knew, two men were dragging me out of the house. I knew they'd started a fire and I kept telling them to rescue my little boy, but they just threw me into the back of a van."

"Why did they start a fire?" I asked. "Was it to destroy evidence?"

"Possibly," said Mum. "More likely they wanted to prove they were a force to be reckoned with, to show how ruthless they could be. It was their way of scaring us into submission."

"We've landed," said the pilot, interrupting the conversation we were so engrossed in. I'd completely forgotten I was on a plane.

"You can disembark now," he said.

Mum and I unbuckled ourselves and took the few paces to the exit door where steps were being wheeled into place. The door swung open and we walked out into the sunshine.

I'd done it! I'd brought Mum home.

Forty
England, the present

Manya hesitated before opening the message, uncertain of what instructions might await her. There was always an undercurrent of manipulation in Papa's plans.

When she saw the photo of Billy standing beside her father in his Moscow office, relief washed over her at Billy's smiling face. But relief was swiftly overshadowed by a wave of fear about Papa's intentions.

The photo was followed by a message which Manya read eagerly, until she reached the condition which made her heart sink.

As you can see, Billy is with me. I will send him back with Galileo on one condition – that you come home immediately.

Manya stared at the stark ultimatum. She didn't want to return to Russia, but she had made too many mistakes. It was time to face the consequences, and try to repair the damage.

She would have to fly back to Moscow.

Neelam had, of course, been overjoyed at the news that Billy was safe but, at the same time, completely mystified. She bombarded Manya with questions.

"Why is Billy in Russia?"

"Who's he with?"

"Is he safe?"

"What has your dad got to do with this?"

Manya tried to answer each question as best she could, without giving away too much. It was essential not to reveal Papa's involvement, and certainly not to let on that she had been caught up in the conspiracy herself. She couldn't bear for Neelam to think badly of her. Luckily, Louis phoned and Manya slunk away, leaving Neelam to her excitement.

"Will you come with me to the airport, Louis? We can bring him home together."

Back in her room, Manya packed up her belongings and said a wistful goodbye to the place she had begun to think of as home. Leaving her bags at the top of the staircase, she went first to the kitchen to thank Gordon for his help and guidance, then she entered the lounge, relieved to find Frank asleep. Gran was sitting with Dardar, gently rocking the doll and singing. Manya went to sit next to her.

"Gran I leave now," she said, feeling tears welling up. "Not come back soon."

"Time for sleep now, my little one," sang Gran, but she took Manya's hand and pressed it against her cheek. She had understood.

"Pssst, come over here," came Beryl's not-so-quiet whisper. "I don't want to wake Frank, the miserable old banana, but I'm going to miss you, girl. Look after yourself and come back to visit, won't you."

Manya could only manage a nod of her head and a teary smile. She'd thought Beryl would be glad to see her leave.

"You are leaving?" said Pasqual, standing up and performing a small bow. Then he glanced around furtively and whispered, "Eh bien, it is very important zat you deliver ze message. Remember, we fight for ze resistance. You won't forget, non?"

Manya smiled at Pasqual, wishing she didn't have to leave. She wouldn't forget. She wouldn't forget any of them. So many months ago, Manya had first come to Autumn Days, completely self-absorbed, narrow-minded and opinionated. Spending time with Neelam, Billy and the Oldies had opened her eyes to new possibilities and a sense of belonging she had never known before.

"Manya, your taxi's here," announced Neelam, wheeling one of the residents into the lounge. "You know you could have come in the car with me and Louis."

Manya preferred to make her own way to the airport. She wasn't sure of Louis's reaction to the whole business and didn't want to risk his hostility. Not when the others had been so generous with their kind farewells.

"I don't understand why you're leaving," continued Neelam. "I wish you weren't, but you know you're welcome back any time. I don't know how the Oldies are going to manage without your Lemon Dribble Cake!"

Manya managed a laugh. The English had a strange sense of humour, but it appealed to her. A country able to joke about serious situations had to be respected.

By the time she arrived at the airport, Manya had resigned herself to the ordeal which lay ahead and the difficult, possibly dangerous tasks she would face.

Having told her father she wouldn't be returning to Moscow until she'd seen Billy and his mum arrive back in England, Manya waited impatiently at the terminal. Mr Molchalin was sending them home in a private jet. Where had his sudden wealth appeared from? And how had Papa managed to send Billy and his mum home from Russia without passports? Did he really have enough influence and power to bypass the usual paperwork?

Suddenly, there it was, the jet from Moscow descending gracefully onto the tarmac. The words 'DM Engineering' were subtly but unmistakeably printed on the fuselage, flaunting Papa's power and newfound wealth. And there was Billy, standing with a woman who must be his mum, at the top of the steps and Manya felt an enormous surge of relief. They were smiling and Manya began to wave, but neither of them saw her because they were already embracing a lady wearing a bright flowery dress and a man wearing running shorts and a t-shirt. Neelam and Louis had arrived to collect them.

Manya held back as though her feet were glued to the tarmac. Billy was laughing, but the shame of her father's actions and Manya's own involvement made her unsure whether to approach the happy group. Would they blame her for everything that had happened? Then she remembered the letter and ran towards Billy.

"Mandy!" he cried, seeing her approach. "Look, this is Mum!"

Billy's mum faced the daughter of the man who had kidnapped her, and she held out her arms. Holding Manya tightly, she whispered in Russian, "Your father told me you're returning to Russia for Billy's sake. I will always be grateful for what you have done. Thank you Manya."

"But it is me who needs say thank you," replied Manya. "Billy is teach me so much."

Manya turned to Billy, handed him the letter and walked slowly towards her father's plane. At the last moment she turned to look back at Billy who was still smiling and waving. Suddenly he ran towards her.

"Don't go Mandy," he said. "Stay with us at Autumn Days."

"I need go, Billy," she said, giving him a tight hug. "But not worry, I come back soon. Is certain."

Epilogue

Mum is brilliant. She wants to live at Autumn Days with the rest of us for now, and certainly until Dad is found. She knew a few things about me from the photos Mandy sent. Mum said it was the photos that kept her going, knowing I was safe and happy.

On the way home in the car, Neelam explained that Mr Molchalin said he would only release me and Mum if Mandy (or Manya, I should start calling her) went back to Russia. Like a swap. I know how much Manya wanted to stay in England, and how much she didn't want to go back to her dad. She'd done the swap for me.

When we arrived at Autumn Days, I couldn't wait for Gran to see Mum. I didn't think she'd recognise her after so many years but, as usual, Gran gave me a big surprise. She looked at Mum and said straightaway,

"Hello Megan, that was a long walk! Did you remember to buy apples?"

When things had calmed down, I opened Manya's letter.

Dear Billy,

I not want go in Russia. Not at all, but I need do this now.

When I back to Russia it is much difficult for me in contact you and impossibility tell you all that happen there. Somebody is going spy on me, listening all my conversation and reading all my message. I am deserving this because is what I once was doing to other people.

I cannot trust Papa, but he need repair his bad, bad choices. It will be much difficulty in finding Zoran and Michael, your papa and take maybe long time, but certainly what I will do. I promise.

Never I stop looking for him. Never.

I want come again in England and I return your papa.

For now, you have much enjoy happy with your mama.

You lucky with living best people I ever meet. I learn so much, but most you Billy, you teach me to be kind.

I very sad for terrible things me and Papa made happen for you and your family, and I hope, one day you much forgive me.

Sorry for bad English. I write never a lot since this language.

For now, until we see once more,

До встречи!

Manya x

THE END

About the author

Caroline is a passionate storyteller, dedicated educator, and proud parent of five wonderful children. With a love for the written word, Caroline has not only inspired students as a teacher but also devised *Crazy Creatives*, a comprehensive course designed to unlock the art of short story writing for aspiring authors of all ages. In 2024, Caroline introduced the first International Short Story Competition, a platform for writers to showcase their talents.

Despite living with multiple sclerosis, Caroline continues to pursue new challenges and adventures, both on and off the page. Supported by her motivational husband, Caroline is embracing a return to the golf course with the goal of competing in the disabled circuit!

If you enjoyed this journey, you won't want to miss

The Runaway Children of Chennai

and

The Secret Children of Mumbai

Coming soon in the Ember Enigmas series...

The Fox of Sevastopol

Followed by ***The Snake of Southwold***

The Chameleon of Carisbrooke

and

The Raven of Paris

www.carolineboxall.com

Instagram: caroline_boxall

Facebook: caroline.boxall

X: @BoxallCaroline

Subscribe to Caroline's blog for a ***FREE SHORT STORY!***

The Secret Life of Dmitri Molchalin

(prequel to The Mole of Moscow)

CarolineBoxall.com

Young Onset Dementia - keeping the flame ignited

Sadly, in my family, we are too familiar with devastating diagnoses – especially young-onset.

Some conditions are thought of as 'old people's illnesses', but when you delve deeper, you find young people suffering with these life-changing diseases.

People say that a person with dementia is a shell of their former self, but within the eyes of each soul is a spark that will never burn out. We just need to know how to keep that flame ignited.

Patrick Ettenes Co-Founder of Bring Dementia Out

Patrick Ettenes is one of the youngest people ever to be diagnosed with a rare form of dementia. Since his diagnosis at 31, Ettenes, (single non-binary) has since become an advocate for raising awareness of early-onset dementia for the LGBTQ+ community, in the hope that no one will have to suffer the isolation and loneliness he faced for all those years.

Thank you, Patrick, for your encouragement in writing *The Mole of Moscow.*

Patrick was awarded Positive Role Model of the Year 2019 and Attitude Magazine: Pride's unsung hero award 2021

Acknowledgements

To my wonderful launch team: your encouragement and support mean everything to me.

Joanne Bryer, Eleanor Dixon, Cheska Tyler, Caron Gent, Emma Roadnight, Margita Hamilton, Gracia Amico, Ann Dawson, Caroline Burrell, Joe Ryan, Robert Taylor, Patsy Collingwood, Pam Barker, Polly Logan, Emma Hill, Jacob Healey, Aaisha Asfiya, Kasey and Carys Senior, Fatima Khakoo, Michelle and Sophie Foy, Shaan Voralia, Natalia and Izzy Rawle, Shanaya Bhalsod, Shrinika Kashyap, Diya and Shaan Bachada, and Insha Dharamsi.

My ever-patient cover designer, Patrick Knowles.

My perceptive and hugely constructive editors, Emily and Katie.

THANK YOU!

Discussion Questions

Character Motivations: How do Billy's and Manya's motivations differ and drive their respective actions throughout the story? Discuss the impact of their backgrounds on their decisions.

Themes of Betrayal and Trust: Betrayal and trust play significant roles in the story. How do these themes manifest in both Billy's and Manya's narratives?

Resilience and Perseverance: How do the characters of Billy and Manya demonstrate resilience and perseverance in the face of adversity? What challenges do they overcome, and how do these challenges shape their development?

Role of Technology: Technology is a recurring element in the story, from Bletchley Park's codebreaking to Manya's hacking. How does technology influence the plot and the characters' actions?

Family Dynamics: Family relationships are complex in the story. How do Billy's and Manya's relationships with their families affect their journeys?

Impact of Historical Context: The story references historical events and places, such as Bletchley Park and Russian codebreakers. How does the historical context enrich the narrative?

Identity and Self-Discovery: Both protagonists go through a journey of self-discovery. How do Billy and Manya's understandings of their identities evolve throughout the story? What key moments contribute to their self-discovery?

Friendship and Allies: Discuss the role of friendships and allies in the story. How do characters like Katie, Louis, and Feliks support or hinder Billy and Manya in their quests?

Ethics and Morality: Manya engages in hacking and other morally ambiguous activities. Discuss the ethical dilemmas she faces and how they affect her character development. Do her actions justify the ends she seeks?

Comparison of Settings: Compare and contrast the settings of Bletchley Park, Autumn Days, and Pushkin Academy. How do these environments influence the characters and the progression of the story?

Conflict and Resolution: The story is filled with conflicts, both internal and external. Are these conflicts resolved by the end of the book?

Plot and Characters: Did you enjoy the book and do you have a favourite character? Caroline would love to know. You can get in touch by emailing: carolineboxall@hotmail.co.uk or via her website: **CarolineBoxall.com**

Creative writing Competition 2025

Enter Caroline's short story competition to win a place in a real, published book!

Rules

- Open to children aged 8-13
- Write a short story with a theme of ***Courage*** in up to 500 words (see tips @ CarolineBoxall.com)
- Edit and improve
- Send your story to CarolineBoxall@hotmail.co.uk by 1st May 2025 (go to CarolineBoxall.com for more details)
- Sign up to the website here where the winners will be announced on 1st June 2025
- NEW: Christmas competition – go to Caroline Boxall.com for details

GOOD LUCK!

Made in the USA
Columbia, SC
19 November 2024

47120920R00167